Information Systems

# GEMINI in an SSADM Environment
## Developing KBS Components

LONDON: HMSO

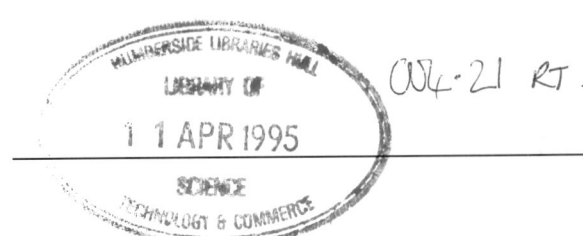

**Acknowledgements**

The assistance of Jim Kennedy and Jennifer Stapleton, under contract to CCTA from Logica UK Ltd is gratefully acknowledged.

© **Crown copyright 1995**

Applications for reproduction should be made to HMSO

First published 1995

ISBN: 0 11 330638 5

**For further information regarding CCTA products please contact:**

CCTA Library
Rosebery Court
St Andrews Business Park
Norwich
NR7 0HS
01603 704704

# Foreword

The Information Systems Engineering Library provides guidance on managing and carrying out Information Systems Engineering activities. In the IS lifecycle, Information Systems Engineering takes place once the IS strategy has been defined. It is concerned with the development and ongoing improvement of information systems up to the operational stage and their maintenance while in operational use.

The Information Systems Engineering Library complements other CCTA products, in particular the project management method, PRINCE and the systems analysis and design method, SSADM.

Volumes in the Information Systems Engineering Library are of interest to varying levels of staff from IS directors to IS providers, helping them to improve the quality and productivity of their development work. Some volumes in this library should also be of interest to business managers, IS users and those involved in market testing whose business operations depend on having effective IS support by means of Information Systems Engineering activities.

The Information Systems Engineering Library also complements other related CCTA products, particularly the Programme and Project Management Library, the Information Management Library for data management issues, the IT Infrastructure volumes for operational issues and the IS Subject Guides for strategic issues.

CCTA welcomes customer views on Information Systems Engineering Library publications. Please send your comments to:

Information Systems Engineering Group
Rosebery Court
St Andrews Business Park
Norwich
NR7 0HS

# Contents

| Chapter | | | Page |
|---|---|---|---|
| 1 | **Introduction** | | 7 |
| | 1.1 | Purpose | |
| | 1.2 | Key messages | |
| | 1.3 | Who should read this publication | |
| | 1.4 | Structure of this publication | |
| | 1.5 | How to use this publication | |
| | 1.6 | Related GEMINI publications | |
| 2 | **Knowledge Based Systems** | | 11 |
| | 2.1 | Introduction | |
| | 2.2 | Handling expertise | |
| | 2.3 | Distinguishing characteristics of KBS | |
| | 2.4 | How to identify potential KBS components | |
| | 2.5 | A KBS or not a KBS: drawing the line | |
| 3 | **Overview of GEMINI concepts** | | 25 |
| | 3.1 | Introduction | |
| | 3.2 | Project organization | |
| | 3.3 | The project management process model | |
| | 3.4 | Products-oriented framework | |
| | 3.5 | Suggested GEMINI activities | |
| | 3.6 | The techniques | |
| | 3.7 | Applying GEMINI | |
| 4 | **Project management issues** | | 37 |
| | 4.1 | Introduction | |
| | 4.2 | A different approach to project management | |
| | 4.3 | Roles in an integrated SSADM project | |
| | 4.4 | Lifecycles and planning | |
| | 4.5 | Project controls | |
| | 4.6 | Project products | |
| 5 | **GEMINI and SSADM: working together** | | 53 |
| | 5.1 | Introduction | |
| | 5.2 | Implications of KBS | |
| | 5.3 | Where to identify KBS in the SSADM project lifecycle | |
| | 5.4 | Interfaces in integrated projects | |
| | 5.5 | Equating products from SSADM and GEMINI | |
| | 5.6 | Relating SSADM and GEMINI activities | |
| | 5.7 | Techniques on KBS projects | |

|   |      | 5.8  | Specialized KBS techniques |     |
|---|------|------|----------------------------|-----|
|   |      | 5.9  | Generally applicable techniques | |
|   |      | 5.10 | Selection of techniques    |     |
| 6 |      | **Skills requirements**    |     | 75 |
|   |      | 6.1  | Introduction               |     |
|   |      | 6.2  | Project controller         |     |
|   |      | 6.3  | Project management         |     |
|   |      | 6.4  | Knowledge engineering      |     |

**Annex**

|   | A    | **Object-orientation and KBS** | 83 |
|---|------|--------------------------------|----|
|   |      | A.1  Introduction              |    |
|   |      | A.2  Object-orientation        |    |
|   |      | A.3  Object-orientation and GEMINI |   |

**Bibliography**    87

**Glossary**    89

**Index**    101

# 1 Introduction

## 1.1 Purpose

This publication is intended to help SSADM project managers to control the integration of knowledge based systems (KBS) elements, produced using GEMINI into a system predominantly developed using SSADM. GEMINI is the CCTA approach to KBS development and SSADM is the CCTA method for the analysis and design of conventional information systems.

GEMINI provides a framework for undertaking KBS development projects; it is not a detailed method and it is applied at a higher level than SSADM. GEMINI defines a set of products to be developed during the analysis and design of KBS and advocates a project management approach which includes PRINCE concepts, tailored for KBS development projects.

This publication will help SSADM practitioners to interpret the GEMINI approach in the context of SSADM Version 4. It draws attention to similarities between GEMINI and SSADM, comparing the concepts used by each, to help the practitioner to relate the two approaches. It indicates where existing SSADM skills can be applied to the KBS elements of the development. At the same time, it identifies the significant differences between the approaches required for the development of KBS and more conventional business systems.

This publication is not intended to give the reader a detailed knowledge of either KBS or GEMINI, but rather to raise awareness of the special issues that need to be addressed during KBS development.

## 1.2 Key messages

The following key messages are emphasized in this publication:

- SSADM allows the incorporation of KBS elements in analysis and design

- Although there are significant differences between KBS and conventional developments, SSADM and GEMINI work together successfully in an integrated development

- Some SSADM techniques can be extended to cover aspects of KBS, but additional techniques are required to address the special requirements of knowledge acquisition and modelling

- The requirement for KBS within a conventional system should be identified early in the project for the GEMINI approach to be applied effectively

- GEMINI can provide useful guidance to SSADM practitioners, but does not give the level of detailed support provided by SSADM. Analysts who lack KBS and GEMINI experience require training before being employed on the development of KBS components.

## 1.3 Who should read this publication

This publication is primarily intended for use by SSADM practitioners, who are likely to be involved in the analysis stages of a conventional system development which has KBS elements. The publication is of prime interest to:

- project managers working on SSADM projects

- SSADM analysts.

The publication is also likely to be of interest to:

- SSADM designers

- GEMINI practitioners.

SSADM designers use their skills in the normal way on an integrated project. This publication provides some assistance in identifying areas where the KBS development is likely to impact on their work, eg additional considerations during capacity planning.

Although this publication is written to suit the SSADM practitioner's perspective, it also sets the context for GEMINI practitioners whose specialist skills are being utilized on an SSADM project with KBS elements. This publication demonstrates some of the inter-relationships between their work and that of the SSADM practitioners.

# Chapter 1
## Introduction

All readers are assumed to be fully conversant with SSADM and PRINCE concepts.

### 1.4 Structure of this publication

Chapter 2 provides an introduction to KBS. If the reader is knowledgeable about KBS, this chapter can be ignored. All other readers should ensure they cover the chapter, since awareness of the ideas and terminology it contains is assumed in subsequent chapters.

Chapter 3 gives an overview of the concepts used in the GEMINI approach to KBS development. This chapter can be ignored by GEMINI practitioners.

Chapter 4 addresses the issues to be considered by the project manager of an integrated SSADM and GEMINI project.

Chapter 5 provides outline assistance in tailoring SSADM to integrate products, activities and techniques from the GEMINI part of the development. Some guidance is provided on the use of SSADM elements in KBS development.

Chapter 6 outlines the skills required and the training needed for personnel to operate effectively in the KBS side of an integrated project.

### 1.5 How to use this publication

This publication should be used in conjunction with the GEMINI volumes of the Information Systems Engineering Library. However, SSADM project managers and practitioners can read it in isolation to gain an insight into the issues to be addressed and the ways to resolve them, when integrating KBS elements into a conventional system.

The publication can be used to determine the skills and/or training required by project staff (both technicians and project managers) involved in the KBS component development.

The publication is intended for use where the KBS development is a GEMINI sub-project within an SSADM project being managed using PRINCE. If the KBS element forms a large proportion of the whole system and this is identified in the early stages of the project, then consideration should be given to managing the whole project using GEMINI and developing the conventional elements of the system in an SSADM sub-project. The publication can be used to gain insight into the relative merits of these approaches in a particular situation.

**1.6 Related GEMINI publications**

The Information Systems Engineering (ISE) Library contains three guides which together form the foundation volumes of the GEMINI guidance. GEMINI provides an approach to the management of development projects for knowledge-based systems (KBS) which can be tailored to suit the needs of individual projects. Many of the concepts embodied in GEMINI can be applied also to non-KBS projects which are innovative or risk-prone or require an iterative approach. Each of the volumes is intended to be self-contained, so some information is duplicated across the volumes. Each volume holds an appropriate level of detail for its purpose and intended audience.

The guides are:

*GEMINI: Controlling KBS Development Projects – Guidance for business-side project controllers*

*GEMINI: Managing KBS Development Projects – Guidance for IS-provider project managers*

*GEMINI Technical Reference – Guidance for KBS development project teams*

# 2 Knowledge based systems (KBS)

## 2.1 Introduction

This chapter provides an introduction to KBS. If the reader is knowledgeable about KBS, this chapter can be ignored. All other readers should ensure they cover the chapter, since awareness of the ideas and terminology it contains is assumed in subsequent chapters.

There is an area of computer science, **Artificial Intelligence (AI)**, which seeks to produce in computer systems behaviour which, if displayed by a human being, would be considered intelligent. One approach has been to incorporate an explicit representation of problem-solving knowledge in computer systems.

The terms **expert systems** and **knowledge based systems (KBS)** are often used interchangeably to describe such systems. KBS tends to have the broader scope since systems which encode knowledge need not necessarily aspire to expert levels of performance. However, for the purposes of this publication, the term **expert** has been retained to denote the individual or individuals whose knowledge is elicited for incorporation in a KBS and **expertise** has been retained to denote the knowledge to be incorporated.

Section 2.2 discusses the issues raised during the handling of expertise in the process of incorporating it into a system.

Section 2.3 discusses the characteristics of KBS which distinguish them from conventional systems.

Section 2.4 gives some guidance on how to identify potential KBS components.

Section 2.5 discusses the delicate judgements to be made on the choice of techniques to determine and represent rules and on whether these rules should be implemented in conventional technology, KBS technology or other innovative technologies.

**2.2 Handling expertise**

The incorporation of expertise in a software system and its application to problem solving raise the following issues:

- how is the expertise acquired? (section 2.2.1)
- how can the expertise be represented? (section 2.2.2)
- how is the expertise applied? (section 2.2.3)

**2.2.1 How is the expertise acquired?**

Conventional IT applications tend to focus on supporting or automating existing flows of information in an organization. KBS focus on supporting or automating the processing of information carried out by individuals. These individuals are usually experts in their respective subjects who can express the pertinent aspects of their reasoning processes and the knowledge they use.

**Knowledge acquisition** is the term commonly applied to the process by which the facts that experts use and the way that they draw inferences from these to solve problems can be identified. The knowledge required from this process is such that a KBS can store it explicitly and apply specific techniques to draw inferences from it.

The main category of knowledge acquisition techniques involves elicitation of the knowledge from experts by the use of interviewing and other techniques. Other categories involve extraction from documents and derivation from data. A mixture of techniques is often appropriate. Knowledge acquisition techniques are discussed more fully in section 8.2 of the *GEMINI Technical Reference*.

**2.2.2 How can the expertise be represented?**

**Knowledge representation** refers to the formalisms that are used to record expertise in a structured form. A vital element in the successful development of KBS is the selection or development of appropriate knowledge representation and inference mechanisms.

Knowledge for use by a KBS may include:

- facts, for example: *John is a doctor*

- rules of thumb, for example: *if you are a grandfather then you are old*

- empirical associations, for example: *people who eat too much get fat*

- ways of dealing with constraints, for example: *if an order can't be met by its due date on the chosen machine then put it on an alternative machine.*

In general, knowledge may be represented in two main classifications:

- **declarative knowledge**, which describes the characteristics and inter-relationships of the objects of interest within the application domain. An example of a piece of declarative knowledge about bank customers could be:

    Customer
    age : 23
    property status : house owner
    in employment : 7 years
    overdrawn in last year : twice

- **problem-solving knowledge**, which describes how to reason with the declarative knowledge. An example of a piece of problem-solving knowledge which uses the declarative knowledge about customers could be a set of rules including the following:

    Rule 1
      IF {customer age} > 20
      and employment status of {customer} is good
      and {customer} is house owner
      and {customer} previous overdrawn < 5 times in
        last year
      THEN {customer} creditworthiness is good

    Rule 2
      IF {customer} in employment > 5 years
      or {customer} employer's reference is good
      THEN employment status of {customer} is good

Knowledge representation techniques are discussed more fully in section 8.3 of the *GEMINI Technical Reference*.

| | | |
|---|---|---|
| 2.2.3 | How is the expertise applied? | Knowledge represented in a KBS is stored in a knowledge base separate from the procedural part of the application. A procedural algorithm, referred to as an inference engine, is used to apply the knowledge to a specific problem. |

In the bank customer example above, the inference engine might be tasked to infer the creditworthiness of a customer. It can do this by searching for a rule which had creditworthiness as its conclusion (rule 1) and attempting to satisfy all its conditions. One of these, *employment status of {customer} is good* would require it to search for a rule with employment status as its conclusion (rule 2). The inference engine can proceed, automatically locating and evaluating rules, until it reaches a conclusion, in this case that the creditworthiness of the customer is good.

Figure 2.1 summarizes the internal structure, inputs and outputs of a KBS. The KBS is presented with the description of a specific problem within the range of problems it is designed to address. The inference engine takes this description and searches for a solution using the knowledge in the knowledge base.

For KBS, even more than for conventional systems, there is a continual need to evaluate the represented knowledge against expert opinion. This, in part, reflects the subjective nature of much of the expertise being represented. KBS present some particularly challenging validation problems. KBS validation techniques are discussed more fully in section 8.4 of the *GEMINI Technical Reference*.

| | | |
|---|---|---|
| **2.3** | **Distinguishing characteristics of KBS** | An important characteristic of KBS is that they provide a mechanism to represent knowledge explicitly within a computer. This characteristic makes it possible to provide the user with meaningful explanations of a problem's solution by making reference to the knowledge used to derive it. Such explanation facilities must still be encoded into the system, but the explicit |

form of the problem-solving processes means that the explanation can be couched in easily understood terms.

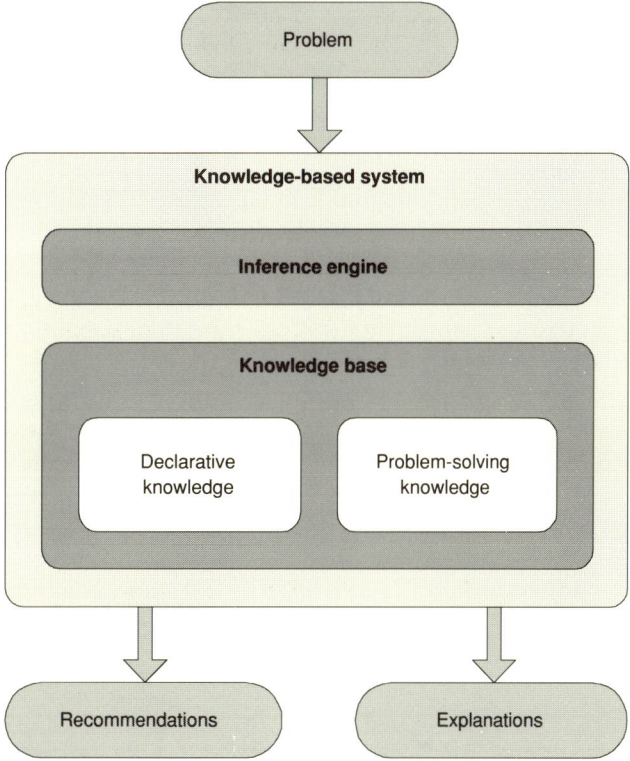

Figure 2.1: The structure of a KBS

So, in the banking example described above, an explanation of why a cheque had been cleared could be provided as:

*The cheque from {customer} has been cleared because they are creditworthy. This is because they are an adult house-owner, with a stable employment status and a good account history.*

This makes KBS particularly appropriate for advisory systems, where the solution often takes the form of recommendations together with explanations of the rationale behind them.

The explicit representation of knowledge also provides flexibility in system maintenance and enhancement, since the individual rules can be inspected to assess the validity of a particular conclusion or the facts upon which it was based.

KBS differ from conventional information systems in the following ways:

- emphasis on **knowledge** which entails subjective interpretation of information

- emphasis on deriving solutions by reasoning, deduction and problem solving rather than data manipulation

- KBS development focuses on extraction of knowledge by asking individuals to examine their reasoning processes.

### 2.4 How to identify potential KBS components

Some KBS are designed as stand-alone systems, but this publication is concerned primarily with those KBS which are integrated into a conventional system. In an integrated development it is necessary to identify those components which need to be analysed and developed as KBS.

#### 2.4.1 The characteristics of KBS components

There is no easy way to identify a potential KBS component but this sub-section provides some general principles and factors to be taken into account.

Given the decision to build a new computer system using SSADM, there is likely to be a business need for a function to be automated or supported. Any activities within this function that currently involve processing of data by skilled or non-clerical staff should be considered as KBS candidates. For example:

- inferring creditworthiness from attributes of a customer

- assessing the tax liability of a customer

- producing a customer profile for marketing.

During the course of an SSADM feasibility study, any Data Flow Diagram (DFD) processes identified which have complex descriptions involving a significant element of decision making, should be considered as possible candidates for KBS.

An example of such a candidate might be a DFD process within a banking cheque clearance system which assesses the creditworthiness of customers whose accounts contain insufficient funds to cover a transaction. This example is illustrated in Figure 2.2.

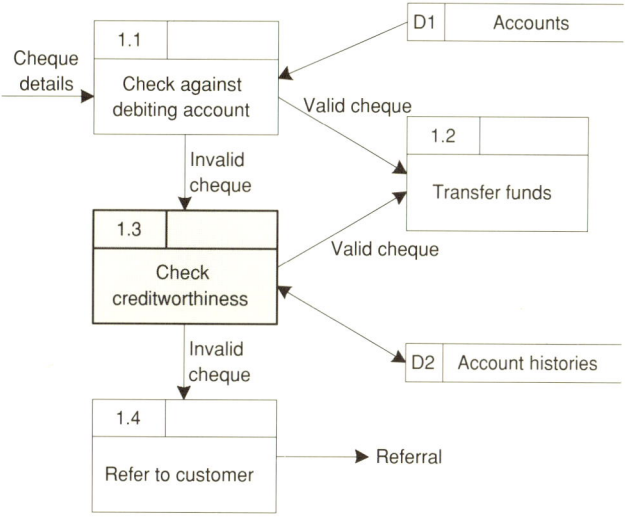

Figure 2.2: A candidate process for KBS

The **Check creditworthiness** process has to perform a complex decision-making task, which takes into account many factors associated with the history of the customer's account. In order to perform this task it is necessary to draw on the expertise of an experienced bank official, perhaps in the form of rules such as:

> *Check the age, employment status, property status and previous account history of the customer. If the customer is over 20 and a house owner, with a good employment status and hasn't been overdrawn more than five times before, then regard them as creditworthy.*

This expertise might be represented in a knowledge base using the forms of knowledge representation described in section 2.2.2.

2.4.2 Evaluating candidate KBS

Given that some such functions are identified, and that clear benefits have already been identified for their automation, it is advisable to evaluate the functions by asking the following questions to assess their suitability as KBS:

- is there expertise?

- is an expert available?

- can the knowledge be represented?

- how stable is it?

Is there expertise?

The primary concern is whether expertise, appropriate to KBS development, actually exists. There are two extremes:

- it may not be possible to perform a particular task at all, since it is not well enough understood, or not currently carried out successfully. A classic example of this is stock-market prediction, where there is no definitive expertise

- the expertise may be too trivial to justify the building of a KBS, eg for routine arithmetical tasks such as calculating interest. In these cases the problem-solving expertise can be supplied by the systems analyst and there is no need to refer to an expert.

The knowledge for the task must be well-bounded if the knowledge acquisition activity is to be controlled. It should not depend too heavily on a broad range of general knowledge.

Very general or common sense knowledge tends to present a problem since it can become difficult to bound the knowledge that the delivered system represents and uses. The problem can be alleviated to some extent by making the system interactive and involving the user's

## Chapter 2
## Knowledge based systems (KBS)

common sense knowledge rather than trying to code it into the application.

As well as the expert's knowledge, information can be obtained from a variety of sources, for example text books, note books and past cases. The availability and accessibility of these sources of knowledge should be considered since they help reduce the demands to be placed on the expert.

Is an expert available?

The availability, enthusiasm and communication skills of the identified expert are of vital importance in developing a KBS.

The developers of the KBS have to be able to acquire the knowledge from an expert within a reasonable timescale. If such an expert cannot be identified, then the chances of success are slim.

One method of establishing whether a suitable combination of expert and expertise exists is called the 'telephone link test'. To assess the feasibility of developing a KBS, an individual must be identified who can formulate approaches for solving problems and, via a telephone conversation, help a novice achieve acceptable levels of performance.

If an expert is identified, then the telephone link test may steer the expert towards an appropriate way of imagining interaction between the potential KBS and the user. If the expert refers to any information sources not arriving from the user over the telephone link then those information sources must also be made available to the KBS.

A good candidate KBS for integration would be one where the expert in the telephone link test makes heavy use of the data to be stored in the data processing part of the system. Such usage helps to maximize the value of that data.

The important role of individual knowledge in a KBS can lead to the more subjective aspects of one expert's opinions being over dominant. KBS developers may need to reconcile the opinions of different experts in order to ensure that the system is generally acceptable.

The expertise involved in the application must be identifiable, appropriate to KBS development and accessible to the development team.

| | |
|---|---|
| Can the knowledge be represented? | If the knowledge involved is not explicable in terms of the classifications in section 2.2.2 then it is unlikely to be tractable to KBS techniques as these are used to represent knowledge in a structured, logical format. Other types of knowledge, such as the subjective interpretation of sensory perceptions, are difficult to represent in a logical structured format, given the current state-of-the-art in KBS. Other kinds of AI approach may be appropriate in these cases. |

The evaluation of an application should include an assessment of both the depth (the level of detail) and breadth (the coverage) of the knowledge to be encoded. In most cases, the preference should be for the development of a deep, narrow knowledge base, rather than a broad, shallow one.

| | |
|---|---|
| How stable is it? | The stability of the knowledge needs to be assessed to determine how quickly the knowledge base will become out of date, and the ramifications that this may have for maintenance of the system. |

The separation of the knowledge base from the inference engine in KBS facilitates the maintenance process since changes to the knowledge base can be made without affecting the rest of the system. However, the effect of the rate of knowledge change should be considered:

- if fast, with changes occurring during implementation, then it is likely that the knowledge base will be out of date before it has been implemented – this is obviously unacceptable

- if moderate, with changes during the lifetime of the system, then the changes could be made, and the alterations will be readily available to all concerned – this may be a great advantage when trying to keep abreast of the latest developments in an area

- if slow, with few changes during the lifetime of the system, then maintenance will be less of an issue. However, it will still be easier to validate the system if it is built around an explicit and separable knowledge base.

## 2.5 A KBS or not a KBS: drawing the line

The preceding sections explore the characteristics of KBS and explain how they can be differentiated from conventional systems. In most cases the differentiation is clear cut but in some cases the dividing line is blurred into a grey area, where subjective judgements have to made on the suitability of competing techniques and the exact partitioning of a system for the use of different techniques.

There are issues of linking from how the expert solves problems to what is implemented in an application, validating the design and ensuring the application's maintainability which affect the choice of:

- acquisition techniques (section 2.5.1)

- representation techniques (section 2.5.2)

- implementation technologies (section 2.5.3).

Often each of these choices can be made independently and while each choice is likely to impinge on the others it does not necessarily dictate them.

### 2.5.1 Acquisition techniques

The degree of dependence on a human individual for the derivation of the problem-solving processes to be incorporated into the system dictates the choice of acquisition techniques. If most of the information can be acquired without directly communicating with or observing the individual, then more conventional analysis techniques may be appropriate. If the analyst needs to spend a large amount of time with an individual over a long period probing complex intellectual processes then KBS knowledge acquisition techniques are more likely to be appropriate.

| 2.5.2 | Representation techniques | KBS representation techniques are only likely to be useful if either KBS acquisition techniques have been used for analysis or KBS technology is to be used for implementation. |
|---|---|---|

There are trends in general software development towards approaches which provide different types of model for the application. The most prevalent and influential of these in relation to potential KBS applications is object orientation. The object-oriented approach has many similarities with the techniques used for modelling knowledge in KBS and may be useful in some cases. Annex A explores this further.

| 2.5.3 | Implementation technologies | The considerations in the choice of implementation technology are ease of implementation, the likelihood of change and performance requirements. Design models which have been determined using knowledge acquisition and representation techniques can often be implemented using conventional technologies. |
|---|---|---|

Types of rules

Rules which need to be implemented in a system can be classified by their degree of inevitability and thus stability. The two extremes of a spectrum are laws of nature and policies:

- **Laws of nature** are rules which encompass immutable truths. For example an equilateral triangle is always a figure with three equal sides and three sixty-degree angles.

- **Policies** are rules made by arbitrary decision which may change according to attitudes or conditions. For example a senior consultant is charged out at £150 an hour. This may change because of prevailing market forces or be negotiable because of the demands on the consultant's time or the amount of time required.

Laws of nature cannot contradict each other. Policies can contradict each other and in extreme cases contradict laws of nature. The closer a rule is to being a law of nature the more reliably it can be implemented. The more arbitrary a policy is the more likely it is to change or be proved inappropriate.

# Chapter 2
## Knowledge based systems (KBS)

KBS technology produces applications in which the rules can be changed fairly readily but KBS are generally slower to run and more difficult to prove than conventional systems. Therefore, changes in policy can be carried out quickly on a KBS with a possible trade off in performance and rigour.

Object-orientation seems to provide a framework within which the different approaches can co-exist. Annex A explores this further.

Embedded rules

Small sets of expert rules within larger systems often perform very specialized tasks which provide very useful functionality but do not perform very complex inferencing. When rule sets are very small and not required to carry out complex inferencing, they can be embedded in the procedural code, rather than being held in a separate rule base and applied by an inference engine.

Clearly this is a subjective judgement and it is difficult to give hard and fast guidelines, but if the inferencing to be carried out is sufficiently complex to require the interaction of multiple rules, then it should be treated as a KBS.

If the main system is heavily dependent on even a small set of rules, whose elicitation from an expert constitutes a substantial knowledge acquisition task then the rules should be implemented in KBS technology.

# 3 Overview of GEMINI concepts

## 3.1 Introduction

This chapter gives an overview of the concepts used in the GEMINI approach to KBS development. GEMINI practitioners will be familiar with the concepts and can go directly to Chapter 4.

The three fundamental characteristics of KBS development projects that prevent conventional methods from fully meeting their needs are:

- special techniques are required

- the activities of feasibility study, requirements definition, analysis and design may overlap

- KBS development projects are generally innovative and thus particularly susceptible to risk

Because of these characteristics, within KBS projects the supply side and the demand side are likely to be operating in separate specialist disciplines with different cultures and languages. These differences often result in a pronounced schism between supply and demand sides, increasing the complexity of project management.

GEMINI sets out the basic principles of an approach to the analysis and design of KBS. It also proposes an approach to those aspects of project control and management which are different in a KBS development project. The characteristics of GEMINI are summarized in the following sections:

- project organization (section 3.2)

- project management process model (section 3.3)

- products-oriented framework emphasizing the products to be generated (section 3.4)

- suggested activities to generate the products (section 3.5)

- the use of specific techniques for representing knowledge (section 3.6).

# GEMINI in an SSADM Environment – Developing KBS Components

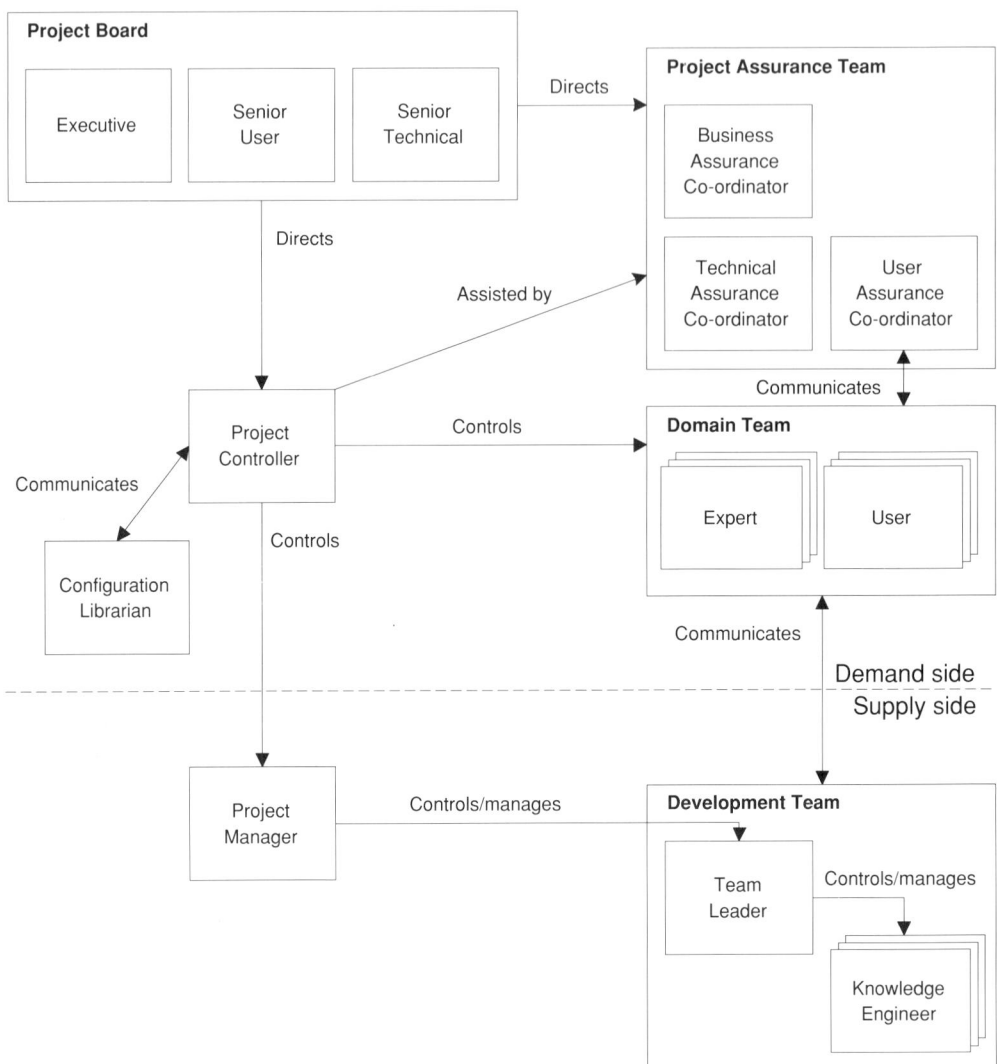

Figure 3.1: GEMINI project organization diagram

Section 3.7 discusses the different ways in which GEMINI can be applied on an integrated project.

**3.2  Project organization**  Within GEMINI, **project organization** is the composition of a team in terms of the skills and experience required to undertake all the necessary functions of control, management and development within a project. The project functions are assigned to a number of designated **roles**. These roles are assigned to individuals according to the needs of the project and the mix of skills available. The roles identified in GEMINI are illustrated in Figure 3.1.

The potential need for a system is established by the demand side. The supply side meets this need by undertaking development of the full KBS, or some aspect of the development.

*GEMINI: Controlling KBS Development Projects*, Chapter 3 addresses the split of roles between the demand and supply sides and details fully the roles and responsibilities within the above organization structure.

The rest of this section gives an indication of the main roles and responsibilities.

3.2.1 Project Board

The **Project Board** is the group of senior managers who have an interest in, and overall control of, the KBS development project. The function and composition of the Project Board are as advocated in PRINCE.

3.2.2 Project Controller

The **Project Controller** is the demand side project manager responsible for the success of the project in terms of quality of the delivered system, within the project's budget and timescale.

It is often difficult to define KBS requirements with sufficient precision to allow accurate estimation of the resources required to meet them. It is, therefore, particularly important that the demand side should retain control over the business organization's resources on the project and make sure that progress towards the requirements is maintained. To ensure that this level of management control is applied the role of Project Controller is given particular prominence in GEMINI.

Ideally, the Project Controller is someone within the user organization with an awareness of KBS development issues, who can act as a translator of requirements and ideas between the demand side and the supply side.

3.2.3 Domain Team

The **Domain Team** is the group of people from the business who have or use the knowledge which the KBS is to contain. The Domain Team provides information for the analysis and design activities carried out by the Development Team.

The two Domain Team roles of particular interest are the User and the Expert.

3.2.4  User

The **User** is the group of users or their representative, who will make direct use of the final implemented system.

3.2.5  Expert

The **Expert** is a group of experts, or their representative, who currently performs the function which the system will eventually provide. The Expert provides the specialist knowledge required by the Knowledge Engineers.

3.2.6  Project Manager

The **Project Manager** has overall responsibility for the management of the supply side activities with additional responsibility for providing information to the demand side.

This role is similar to the standard PRINCE Project Manager role, except that liaison with the Project Board is conducted through the Project Controller.

3.2.7  Development Team

A Project Manager is supported by at least one **Development Team** which is responsible for delivering the products of the project. These roles have the same overall function as a development team on a non-KBS project. Different skills are required to undertake these functions which relate directly to the techniques and technology being employed.

The **Team Leader** has to manage the development of particular products using specified resources.

**Knowledge Engineers** are the main body of development personnel in a KBS development project. They carry out the analysis, design and programming activities.

## 3.3 The project management process model

The project management process model incorporates the management of risk because KBS developments are more threatened by risks than many conventional developments. It also takes account of the iterative nature of KBS development.

*GEMINI: Controlling KBS Development Projects*, Chapter 4 recommends that a KBS development project should be regularly reviewed, and if necessary re-planned. After each review, a risk assessment should be carried out to consider all issues which could jeopardize the success of the project and assess the necessity for re-planning.

Risk is defined as the likelihood and impact of the system **failing** to:

- meet a business need and hence of its not providing its expected business benefits

- prove technically feasible

- prove organizationally feasible

- be completed on time and within budget

- develop products which meet requirements.

A GEMINI project always begins with an initial review of the project objectives and an initial analysis of the risk inherent in undertaking the project. A first project plan should then be produced, identifying the major project deliverables, the activities to produce them and the control points.

The project is carried out as an initial review followed by a sequence of project management processes:

**risk assessment – planning – development – review**

The term development is used to refer to the technical activities that make up the project and includes analysis and design as well as implementation.

Each iteration of the sequence should yield progress in:

- degree of understanding of outstanding risk
- accuracy of future plans and estimates
- development of the implementable KBS
- quality, that is, assuring the fitness for purpose of products

This iteration of the project management process sequence can be represented graphically as a spiral. A passage through all four sectors comprises a circuit of the spiral. This is shown in Figure 3.2

Figure 3.2: Project management process control

GEMINI has **control points** when development work is stopped, progress is assessed and the remainder of the project defined. These control points are co-ordinated with completion of deliverables and other critical events. Each circuit of the spiral equates to a PRINCE stage or the part of a stage between end-stage and mid-stage control points. The review, risk assessment and planning sectors of the spiral replace PRINCE mid-stage and end-stage assessments.

On a large project, the Project Controller creates a second-level spiral for each major activity of the project. Since activities may be carried out concurrently, several of these spirals may be operative at any one time. Each second-level spiral consists of an initial review followed by the cycle of risk assessment, planning, development and review. The spirals are subordinate to the project-level spiral and must be co-ordinated with it.

Where appropriate, activities may be divided into sub-activities and lower-level spirals created, feeding information to higher levels. The degree of project control can be varied by the number of spirals created at each level, the number of circuits in a spiral and the formality of documentation for each level.

## 3.4 Products-oriented framework

*GEMINI Technical Reference*, Chapter 4 recommends the set of products which should be produced on a KBS development project. This set is divided into three categories:

- **Management Products,** which are used in the management of the project and focus on planning and control aspects

- **Quality Products,** which show that quality has been built into the process of developing the system

- **Technical Products,** which are the results of the project development activities. Some of the Technical Products, for example Education Products, do not directly contribute to the developed KBS. The products normally associated with the development of the system, including analysis, design and implementation products are grouped into the **Application Products**.

*GEMINI Technical Reference*, Chapter 5 contains exemplar product descriptions which can be developed into a full set appropriate to each project.

The eight models described below are the **Application Products** which are the major deliverables of a GEMINI project. Each model is the encapsulation of some key aspect of the system.

### 3.4.1 Business Domain Model

The **Business Domain Model** is a representation of the enterprise, giving an understanding of the organizational structure and business function. For potential applications, the Business Domain Model covers both current and proposed systems and requirements.

### 3.4.2 Application Requirements Model

The **Application Requirements Model** holds a specification of the required external behaviour of the system, together with the organizational, operational, technical and resource constraints which affect the way that the system is to be designed and implemented.

### 3.4.3 Selected Application Model

The **Selected Application Model** is a representation of the tasks and data flows in an application. This representation provides a more precise definition of the functionality of the proposed application than the Business Domain Model.

### 3.4.4 Expertise Model

The **Expertise Model** holds a description of the knowledge (expertise) to be encoded into the implemented KBS.

### 3.4.5 Modality Model

The **Modality Model** defines the agents in the proposed system and their way of interacting with each other. Agents are persons or other systems that interact with, or are components of, the proposed system. The Modality Model defines the agents, the tasks each performs and how they interact. It models when the agents can ask for or give information. The pattern of interaction between agents is known as modality.

### 3.4.6 Logical Analysis Model

The **Logical Analysis Model** brings together the Expertise Model and the Modality Model into a single validated whole. The expert and user views of the application are drawn together and cross-validated to ensure that a coherent specification is built for the application. It is the pivotal product in a GEMINI project.

## Chapter 3
## Overview of GEMINI concepts

3.4.7 Functional Design Model

The **Functional Design Model** is a revision of the Logical Analysis Model. The revision reflects design decisions concerning how individual components of the system are to be implemented. The model is independent of any particular implementation environment.

3.4.8 Physical Design Model

The **Physical Design Model** provides a representation of all the components and functions of the system to be implemented. It is implementation-dependent, the design details being dependent on the technical environment chosen for implementation.

**3.5 Suggested GEMINI activities**

GEMINI does not stipulate the activities that should be undertaken to generate the products. It merely requires that an appropriate set of activities be defined which takes into account the order in which the products are required and any dependencies existing between them. This is consistent with the PRINCE (and SSADM) concept of producing Product Descriptions, Product Flow Diagrams and then Activity Networks. To illustrate this, an example set of top-level GEMINI activities is shown:

| Activity | Major Products |
| --- | --- |
| Feasibility Study | Feasibility Report (which includes initial versions of some of the products below) |
| Requirements Analysis | Business Domain Model, Application Requirements Model |
| System Modelling | Selected Application Model |
| Logical Analysis | Expertise Model, Modality Model, Logical Analysis Model |
| Logical Design | Functional Design Model |
| Technical Environment Definition | Technical Environment Description, Application Requirements Model |
| Physical Design | Physical Design Model |

Figure 3.3: An example set of top-level GEMINI activities and products

# GEMINI in an SSADM Environment – Developing KBS Components

*GEMINI Technical Reference*, Chapter 7, further sub-divides the suggested activities into example Steps.

## 3.6 The techniques

*GEMINI Technical Reference*, Chapter 8 provides an outline description of techniques which can be used on a KBS development project. The techniques cover the full range of requirements capture, analysis and design.

KBS projects typically use a greater diversity of techniques and tools than conventional systems projects. GEMINI supports this diversity by providing a framework into which practitioners can fit the techniques and skills they already employ. It is important, therefore, that the selection of techniques is explicitly considered and that decisions are reviewed critically throughout the project.

Techniques are split into two categories:

- generally applicable techniques
- KBS specific techniques.

The KBS specific techniques are considered in three areas:

- knowledge acquisition
- knowledge representation
- KBS validation.

The choice of knowledge representation technique is of particular importance in a KBS development project, since it can constrain the physical implementation.

KBS validation addresses the continual need to evaluate the represented knowledge against expert opinion. Because KBS present some particularly challenging validation problems, GEMINI concentrates on KBS specific validation and testing techniques. However, KBS development projects also make use of the full range of conventional testing techniques, for example inspection, unit testing, integration testing and regression testing.

## 3.7 Applying GEMINI

This publication assumes that a KBS element has been identified within a conventional systems development resulting in an SSADM project, managed using PRINCE, which contains a GEMINI sub-project. The GEMINI project is set up part way through the PRINCE/SSADM project, operates in parallel to the main project and is integrated back into it at an appropriate time.

In some circumstances, it may be more appropriate to give GEMINI either a greater or lesser role than is assumed.

### 3.7.1 GEMINI with a greater role

GEMINI should have a greater role when the KBS element either forms a large proportion of the proposed system and this is identified in the early stages of the project, or is fairly ill-defined. Sometimes the whole project can benefit from an iterative development approach. In this case the whole project should be run within the GEMINI framework and the conventional elements of the system should be developed in an SSADM sub-project. *GEMINI: Controlling KBS Development Projects*, Chapter 9 gives more information on integrating conventional IT systems development within a GEMINI project.

### 3.7.2 GEMINI with a lesser role

GEMINI should have a lesser role when the KBS element is small, comparatively straightforward and is well bounded and defined. In this case some of the GEMINI concepts and KBS techniques may be incorporated into an SSADM project without setting up a separate GEMINI sub-project. Some guidance on where this may be useful is now given in respect of the KBS characteristics that GEMINI addresses:

- special techniques are required

- the activities of feasibility study, requirements definition, analysis and design may overlap

- KBS development projects are generally innovative and thus, particularly susceptible to risk

- the schism between supply and demand sides.

| | |
|---|---|
| Special techniques | If the critical characteristic of the identified KBS component is the need to use special techniques, then KBS products and the activities to produce them can be added to the SSADM products and activities and specified within the PRINCE method. More information on this is given in Chapter 2. |
| Overlapping activities | If the critical characteristic of the identified KBS component is the need to overlap activities, then the role of GEMINI will depend on how well the work involved in developing the KBS component can be scoped. If there is confidence that the work can be completed satisfactorily within a specific timescale or to coincide with relevant SSADM products and activities, then the concepts of the spiral model can be applied within a PRINCE stage, using parallel processes without setting up a formal GEMINI sub-project. |
| Risk | If the critical characteristic of the identified KBS component is risk, then the mid-stage and end-stage assessments of the PRINCE stage can be set accordingly and the products and activities of the review, risk assessment and planning sectors of the spiral can be incorporated into the stage. |
| Supply/demand split | If the critical characteristic of the identified KBS component is the schism between supply and demand sides, then the appropriate GEMINI roles can be incorporated into the PRINCE organizational structure for the duration of the relevant stage. |
| Summary | Decisions on which concepts of GEMINI apply are dependent on the characteristics of the KBS components and their role within the overall development. Therefore, prescriptive guidance cannot be given on what to apply where. However, this chapter gives the issues to be addressed and some indication of the criteria to be used. |

# 4 Project management issues

## 4.1 Introduction

This chapter discusses the project management issues involved in conducting a project as an SSADM project under PRINCE when there are KBS elements to be developed using GEMINI.

Section 4.2 discusses the special characteristics of the GEMINI approach to project management, with the emphasis on risk assessment and iterative development.

Section 4.3 covers the additional roles required by GEMINI.

Section 4.4 compares the different underlying process models and their potential impact on project planning.

Section 4.5 discusses project controls including quality and configuration management controls.

Section 4.6 covers products and their control.

## 4.2 A different approach to project management

The GEMINI approach to project management is based on PRINCE but places particular emphasis on certain aspects.

### 4.2.1 How is the emphasis different?

In order to increase the likelihood of developing a successful KBS, the GEMINI guidance:

- recommends a flexible project control framework which makes explicit allowance for re-planning

- places emphasis on the management of risk

- recommends the additional project management role of Project Controller to control the interface between supply and demand organizations

- recognizes the need for additional techniques and products for knowledge representation which are not necessary in non-KBS developments.

GEMINI provides less direct support than SSADM for control of analysis and design, in that:

- it does not specify activities
- it does not link techniques or activities closely to products.

### 4.2.2 Why is the emphasis different?

These differences in emphasis are related to three fundamental characteristics of KBS projects:

- KBS projects are generally innovative and thus more susceptible to risk
- the activities of feasibility study, requirements definition, analysis and design typically overlap in KBS projects
- special techniques are required for knowledge acquisition and representation.

*Risk in KBS projects*

Generally the full definition of the functionality of KBS can be achieved only after a period of knowledge acquisition with an expert. The acquisition of knowledge is often more difficult than the acquisition of requirements associated with conventional projects. This coupled with the use of innovative techniques increases the probability of missed delivery and budget targets.

Risk analysis and re-planning should be made much more explicit in the project control process. The emphasis on risk analysis in GEMINI is part of the reason for the adoption of a spiral lifecycle model.

*Overlapping activities in KBS projects*

Since the functionality of the system can only be fully defined after knowledge acquisition, it is not possible to separate the processes of analysis, design and implementation in a clean linear sequence. Some revision of the design and even the analysis products may occur late in the project as the scope and limitations of the expert's knowledge emerge. It may be necessary to revise the assessment of the feasibility and scope of the system at a relatively late stage in the project.

These activities may therefore overlap to a degree not normally expected in the staged development of a specific area of functionality using SSADM. Comparison of the phasing of KBS development against that of a normal SSADM development is shown in Figure. 4.1.

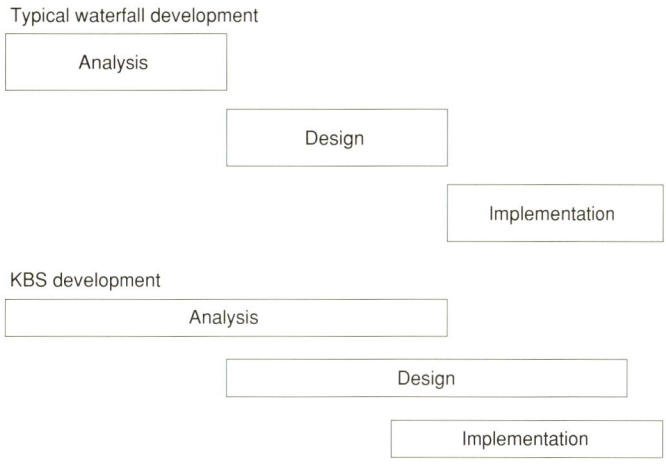

Figure 4.1: Comparison of development stages

Another way that GEMINI characterizes the overlap of activities is by acceptance of incomplete models as products. Models can be developed in parallel provided that the interdependencies are allowed for and completeness criteria are identified for assessment of the state of completion of a model. Figure 4.2 illustrates GEMINI models in various states of completeness.

An incomplete model developed to predefined criteria is a discrete technical product. GEMINI uses a product-based approach to project management to maintain control of the incomplete models and the overlapping iterative activities. PRINCE stages are identified from the Activity Network arising from the Product Flow Diagram and usually reflect the delivery of a number of complete products.

Special techniques for knowledge acquisition.

The incorporation of expert knowledge in KBS requires special techniques and forms of representation. The techniques which are currently used to define these representations are less formalized than conventional

# GEMINI in an SSADM Environment – Developing KBS Components

software engineering techniques and rely heavily on the skills of interpreting the results of informal interviews with experts.

Figure 4.2: Various states of completeness of the key GEMINI development models

GEMINI products are not currently linked to techniques and notations in the way that is defined in core SSADM.

## 4.3 Roles in an integrated SSADM project

All the normal roles in a conventional project are required, but important additional roles are needed for the KBS development:

- Project Controller
- Expert
- Knowledge Engineer.

## Chapter 4
## Project management issues

**4.3.1 The Project Controller**

An additional component of the project management structure is the Project Controller. In a GEMINI project the Project Controller is the demand side project manager for the KBS development. The Project Controller provides close links between the project team and the Project Board members and attends Project Board meetings. The Project Controller, who controls the resources of the demand side, is the liaison point between demander and supplier and is responsible to the demand side authority for the success of the project in terms of quality of the delivered system, budget and timescale.

In an integrated project, a Project Manager who, in respect of the KBS element, can represent demander interests and control demander resources may perform this role. If the Project Manager cannot represent the demander in this way or the project size and riskiness warrant it, a separate Project Controller must be appointed. The role and responsibilities of the Project Controller are explained in *GEMINI: Controlling KBS Development Projects*, Annex A.

**4.3.2 The Expert**

The Expert may be a group of experts or their representative who is available for interview to obtain detailed understanding of the knowledge that is to be incorporated in the KBS.

**4.3.3 The Knowledge Engineer**

The Knowledge Engineer is responsible for extracting and encoding the Expert's knowledge. This often requires a broad range of skills suitable for the performance of any task from analyst to programmer level, since the best notation for recording knowledge may well be a KBS-oriented programming language or specific prototyping tool. The circumstances under which prototyping may be used in this way are discussed further in section 4.6.2.

**4.3.4 The KBS development team**

The broad skill base of the Knowledge Engineer and the incremental nature of the development under GEMINI create a mismatch between the concept of SSADM Module Team and the GEMINI development team(s). There should probably be one team for the entire KBS development.

If the KBS component is small, one project team member may perform all the KBS activities. Since the activities of the GEMINI practitioner impact the activities of the SSADM practitioners and vice versa, the GEMINI practitioner should report to the relevant SSADM Stage or Module Manager.

With a larger KBS component, it may be necessary to have a KBS Team Leader or KBS Project Manager reporting to the overall Project Manager in the same way as SSADM Module and Stage Managers. Close contact should be maintained with the SSADM Module and Stage Managers to ensure that the products and activities progress in step across the development teams.

### 4.4 Lifecycles and planning

The project management process model in GEMINI presents a very different appearance to the more conventional type of lifecycle which is commonly associated with SSADM. The two lifecycles are actually compatible but they have different emphases for project management and control as illustrated in the following sections.

The differences can best be illustrated by considering, in outline, how project planning is carried out in an SSADM project under PRINCE and in a GEMINI project.

### 4.4.1 SSADM/PRINCE planning

PRINCE defines three types of plan – Technical, Resource and Exception. Quality aspects are defined within the Technical and Resource Plans. At the outset of a project the Technical Plan is generated by:

- identifying a series of Stages. In an SSADM environment, this also effectively defines the products to be generated, since products are closely linked to Stages

- defining Mid and End Stage Assessments, which are the PRINCE control points. Progress on the project will be monitored at these and corrective action taken where necessary.

A Resource Plan is then generated to allocate resources to achieve the Technical Plan. An Exception Plan is generated whenever an exception situation has arisen or is likely to arise.

The Technical Plan tends to have a linear appearance as illustrated in Figure 4.3:

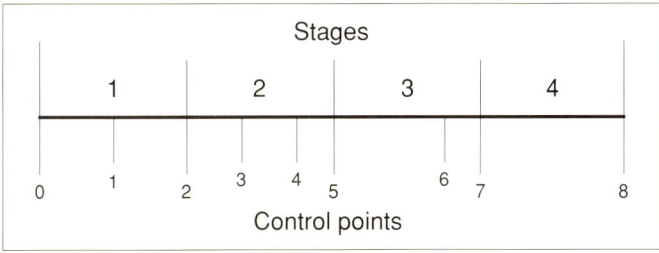

Figure 4.3: PRINCE technical plan

### 4.4.2 GEMINI Planning

GEMINI makes the quality aspects of plans explicit to emphasize the importance of planning for quality. All plans have technical, resource and quality aspects and initial planning is carried out to:

- identify the major project products to be generated
- define a set of activities to generate those products
- define control points
- relate the project products, activities and control points to spiral circuits
- allocate resources.

Control points are generally to be expected at project initiation, completion of the Feasibility Study, completion of both Requirements Analysis and System Modelling, completion of Logical Analysis, completion of the Logical Design, completion of the Technical Environment Description and completion of the Physical Design. Other control points should be defined according to the specific circumstances of the project. Progress on the project is monitored at these control points and corrective action taken where necessary.

In terms of the GEMINI project management process model, the resultant plan corresponds to that which is produced during the planning sectors of the first loop of the spiral demonstrated in Figure 4.4 and has a similar form to the corresponding PRINCE plan.

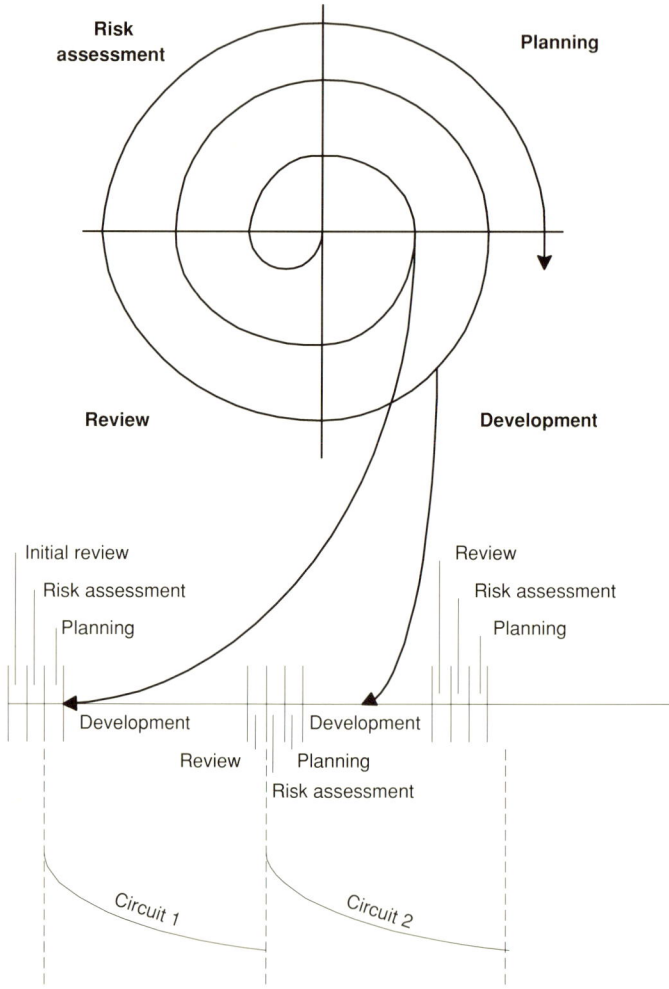

Figure 4.4: A spiral view of a project

The spiral model relates the management activities of review, risk assessment and planning to the development activities. Each plan and review must be related to the activities and products of the adjacent development

# Chapter 4
## Project management issues

sector. It identifies where and how to monitor and control project progress. The development activities are carried out within successive development sectors of the spiral. Figure 4.4 demonstrates that the sectors of the spiral consume differing amounts of resource.

If the project (or sub-project) is planned using a single spiral then it is possible to unwind the spiral so that the circuits represent PRINCE stages or part stages. The interacting hierarchy of spirals which commonly characterizes the use of GEMINI complicates any linear representation.

4.4.3 Differences between GEMINI and SSADM/PRINCE

The principal differences in emphasis between GEMINI and SSADM/PRINCE applied to the planning of a project are:

- GEMINI defines products without stipulating the default Stages and Steps to be undertaken to generate them, but it does give some examples. The activities to be used must therefore be derived and defined for each project. While some tailoring of SSADM products and activities may be necessary, the default set is well defined and established

- SSADM/PRINCE reviews occur at the end of stages. In GEMINI, control points are linked to circuits of spirals and activities which may produce incomplete models

- GEMINI places great emphasis on the management of risk and recommends an explicit allowance of time and effort for the risk analysis activity at each control point. Where a large or highly critical KBS component is present it may be advisable to adopt the GEMINI approach to the management of risk for the whole project

- GEMINI addresses explicitly the split between the demand and supply sides and identifies additional roles required to bridge the differences in culture.

If, during the course of the project, it becomes necessary to re-plan then it is likely that the same corrective measures will be adopted by either approach.

4.4.4 Management of risk

In principle, the KBS component can be treated as just another system component and the work on it planned as usual. In practice, however, the increased risk associated with the KBS component has the following impact on project planning and control:

- more frequent re-planning may be required than would normally be the case

- typically, to minimize re-planning, a much more intensive feasibility study is required for the KBS components than for the non-KBS components. This may involve extensive knowledge acquisition sessions and may require an extended time period.

The uncertainty of success which is introduced into the project when a KBS component is required may have serious implications if that component is not identified until a late stage in the project, eg late in Requirements Specification. In this case, work may have to be suspended while the feasibility of the KBS component is assessed and the future development of the non-KBS components is re-planned. For this reason it is vitally important to identify KBS components and assess their criticality to the system as early as possible in the project.

4.4.5 Scheduling

A major concern in planning an integrated project is the scheduling of the activities associated with the KBS and non-KBS components of the system. Like PRINCE and SSADM, GEMINI is products-oriented but, unlike SSADM, it is not as helpful in detailing activities to deliver those products. A set of activities should, therefore, be defined for the KBS components which takes into account the dependencies between the products being generated by SSADM and GEMINI.

Some of the key dependencies between the GEMINI and SSADM products (Stage 3 onwards) are shown in Figure 4.5. The diagram illustrates some of the likely dependencies in an example project. Any dependencies must be identified according to the relationship between the KBS and non-KBS components of the system. The direction of a dependency between two products is indicated by the head of the arrow, with mutual dependencies represented by double arrows. For the sake of clarity, the diagram shows a reduced set of products. All products are dependent on the SSADM Requirements Catalogue.

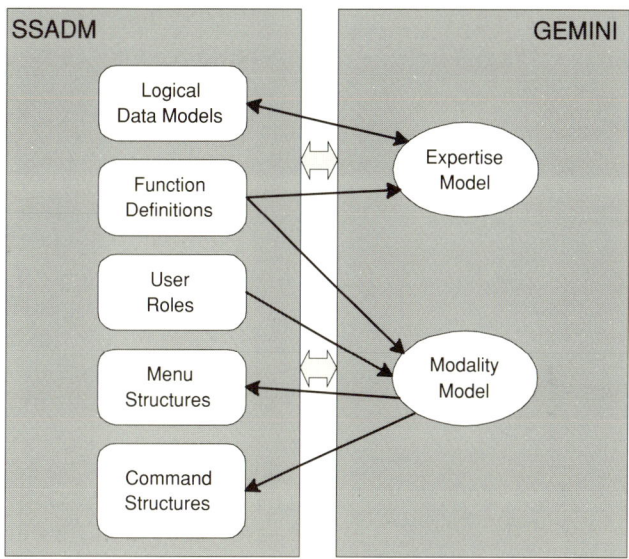

Figure 4.5: An example of some dependencies between products in an integrated project

4.4.6 Integrated plan generation

The process of generating a plan for an integrated project can be summarized by the following sequence of activities:

1 Align the products to be generated by SSADM and GEMINI to take into account the dependencies for the project.

2 Define a set of activities for the KBS components to generate the products in the required order and identify the control points at which they will be reviewed.

3 Schedule the SSADM and GEMINI activities to maintain the product dependencies.

The exact relationships between the activities will depend on the particular project and the extent to which progress on the SSADM products depends on the KBS products.

An example of an activity network is shown in Figure 4.6. A directed link between a pair of activities indicates that the activity at the arrow head cannot be completed until the activity at the other end is completed. In this example the KBS activities are heavily dependent on the SSADM activities. In other projects it is possible that SSADM activities such as selection of Technical System Options will depend on knowing the demands placed by the KBS in which case the arrow between those activities would be reversed.

This diagram shows strict dependencies between activities. An appropriate level of communication should be maintained between all the SSADM and GEMINI activities even where there is no direct dependency.

4   If the KBS components are likely to be large or critical to the performance of the system, allow for a large GEMINI Feasibility Study before committing resources to the project. In practice it is likely that much of the detailed knowledge acquisition will actually be carried out during the Feasibility Study and this will form the basis of the final system. In the extreme case, where a high level KBS tool is being used, the subsequent activities of analysis and design may be relatively trivial. The effect on the overall project plan will typically be to extend the feasibility stage and concentrate much of the KBS effort early in the project.

5   Make an explicit allowance in the plan for the time and effort required to carry out risk analysis and re-planning, if required, at the control points.

# Chapter 4
# Project management issues

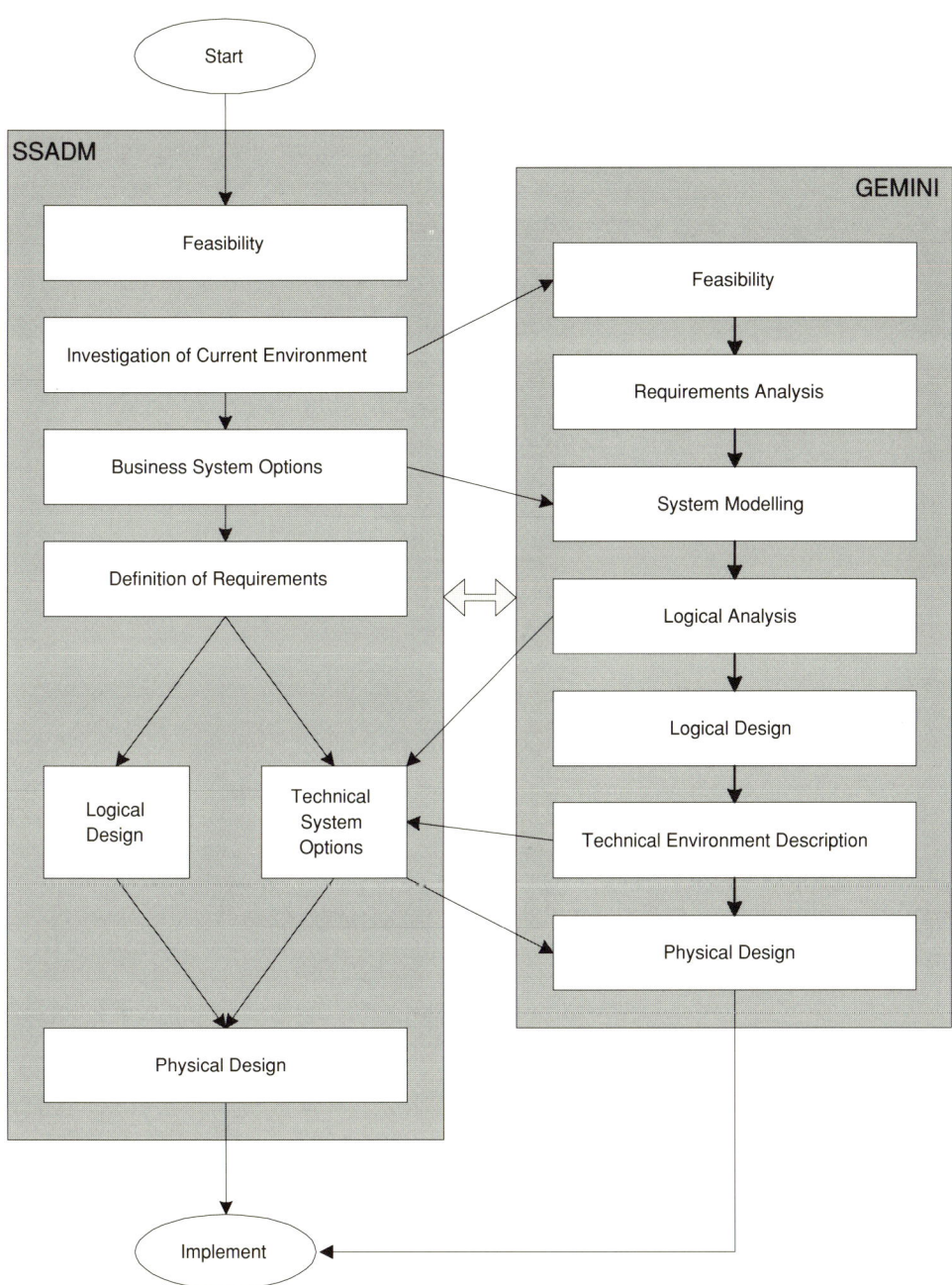

Figure 4.6: A sample activity network for an integrated project

**4.5** **Project controls**  This section discusses the management and project control issues in an integrated project.

4.5.1  Management Controls

Clearly, project initiation and closure are common to both parts of the integrated project. The difference in control points is in the body of the development. In GEMINI, controls are exercised within the review, risk assessment and planning sectors of each spiral. Assessing the problem-solving capability of the KBS is an important activity required by GEMINI. Although this can be tested during development, it cannot be judged fully until the KBS components are in operation. If the KBS components prove unsatisfactory, further GEMINI work may be required. It is likely that any problems will be local to the KBS components and will not impact on the SSADM deliverables.

Problems of control are likely to be more severe the later the identification of a KBS component, since part of the project must return to feasibility study mode to assess the KBS component. As described in section 4.4, the assessment of the feasibility of KBS makes intensive use of resources which can severely impact on the development of the non-KBS components.

The problem should be addressed according to the stipulated PRINCE procedures. This involves raising a Project Issue Report and thence an Exception Report. Appropriate Exception plans have to be developed and presented to the Project Board. The Project Board then has to decide whether or not to put the project on hold while the KBS feasibility study is carried out, depending on several factors, including the criticality of the potential KBS component and when the KBS is required.

4.5.2  Product controls

Quality criteria for products in SSADM are laid down in the Product Descriptions which facilitate the quality review process. In GEMINI, since the products are only loosely defined in terms of their content, quality attributes will need to be derived for each product not covered by an SSADM Product Description.

Most SSADM products are only placed under configuration control when they have met all the quality control criteria in their Product Descriptions. Similarly a

# Chapter 4
# Project management issues

PRINCE product which forms part of the delivered system is a configuration item. GEMINI models can be placed under configuration management at various stages of completeness. The models are developed at different rates and consistency between them has to be maintained. A GEMINI product may be defined as a particular model at a defined state of completeness which must be documented, together with the relevant quality criteria.

**4.6 Project products**

Section 5.4.1 provides correspondences between the technical GEMINI and SSADM products and identifies umbrella technical products which span the two branches of development. The objectives of the corresponding products are similar but the contents of the GEMINI products are different from the SSADM ones.

**4.6.1 Management products**

The management products are largely specified by PRINCE but the emphasis may well be different and additional relevant GEMINI products should be introduced, either specific to the GEMINI sub-project or incorporated into suitable PRINCE products. In the latter case the PRINCE Business Risk Management Checklist is likely to contain a seemingly high proportion of KBS risks when the size of the KBS component is compared with that of the SSADM component (see Chapter 6 and Annex D of *GEMINI: Controlling KBS Development Projects* for information on risk management).

**4.6.2 Controlling technical products**

SSADM implies that a product must be verified as suitable for input to dependent products before their development can take place. In practice, partial products can be used as input to subsequent products in the development. This is formalized in GEMINI by explicitly allowing both the overlap of activities which can take place in the project and the production of partial models.

An activity which has had greater prominence in KBS development is prototyping. In core SSADM, prototyping is defined only at Step 350 Develop Specification Prototypes where the specification is checked (although in practice SSADM projects often prototype whatever and wherever is appropriate). In KBS development, prototyping is very common indeed and covers more areas than the user interface.

As stipulated in the ISE Library volume: *Prototyping in an SSADM Environment*, the general rule in prototyping is only to build prototypes for specific purposes. In KBS projects, prototyping is used particularly to demonstrate proposed functionality and address areas of technical risk. One purpose of prototyping in KBS development is to allow the Expert to decide whether or not the knowledge is being correctly interpreted in the knowledge base.

Since the knowledge base is the foundation of any KBS it is tempting to develop a prototype further to produce the finished KBS, rather than discarding it and rebuilding from scratch. The benefits of developing a prototype knowledge base further should be examined critically before making this decision. GEMINI recommends that:

> *Prototyping should not be allowed to pre-empt design decisions. It is preferable to build prototypes with the intention that they will be discarded rather than form the direct basis of further development.*

# Chapter 5
# GEMINI and SSADM: working together

## 5 GEMINI and SSADM: working together

### 5.1 Introduction

This chapter provides guidance for SSADM practitioners on the use of GEMINI in support of SSADM on a project which involves the integrated development of KBS within a larger system development.

Section 5.2 describes the implications of KBS for an integrated system project.

Section 5.3 provides guidance on where to identify KBS components in the SSADM project lifecycle.

Section 5.4 describes the interfaces between SSADM and GEMINI on an integrated project.

Section 5.5 discusses the relationships between products from SSADM and GEMINI.

Section 5.6 discusses the relationships between activities in SSADM and GEMINI.

Section 5.7 discusses the techniques employed on integrated projects.

Section 5.8 describes the types of specialized KBS techniques.

Section 5.9 identifies generally applicable techniques which may be used on KBS development projects.

Section 5.10 discusses the selection of techniques on a project.

### 5.2 Implications of KBS

The integration of a KBS development into a conventional system development has implications for the design of the overall technical solution. This section describes those implications under the following:

- the ways in which the technical approach differs (section 5.2.1)

- the factors determining the impact of KBS on the integrated system (section 5.2.2)

# GEMINI in an SSADM Environment – Developing KBS Components

- the interfaces to KBS in an integrated system (section 5.2.3).

### 5.2.1 How the technical approach is different

SSADM is intended for use in the analysis and design of software systems which are primarily data based. Traditionally such data processing systems would replace some paper-based manual system for managing, recording and transporting information around an organization.

A key feature of KBS is the emphasis on solving some problem by emulating the reasoning carried out by individuals who are capable of solving the problem in question. Often this reasoning is logical rather than arithmetical and can be characterized as rules.

KBS therefore require a different technical approach, which is characterized by:

- explicit knowledge acquisition activities

- dependence on experts in the domain of the application

- special user interface requirements

- the use of specialized tools.

#### Knowledge acquisition

Because a successful KBS is dependent on emulating an appropriate part of a person's expertise, the first priority is to identify the knowledge they use to solve a problem. Once a good picture is built up of the knowledge and data used and the inferences an expert makes using it, it is then possible to assess how easy this might be to emulate. The best domains for KBS are those that use a well defined and bounded body of specialist knowledge.

In order to extract the knowledge, much of which may be subjective and deep seated, it is necessary to supplement the standard systems analysis techniques with techniques derived from the field of cognitive psychology. The aim of these techniques is to help the person involved to express the problem solving knowledge they are using.

Specialist knowledge is the knowledge particular to the expert's field of endeavour as opposed to general knowledge which non-specialists share. If it becomes apparent that the expert is continually referring to general knowledge then it is likely to be difficult to contain the system. For example an expert giving medical advice might make use of common-sense facts about people and their lifestyles in the course of a consultation. By contrast the specific symptoms that an expert associates with a disease are likely to be well bounded.

In some cases KBS developers proceed by directly prototyping the knowledge as it is acquired. This allows some of its implications and inconsistencies to be explored and fed back to the expert for comment or resolution. Building prototypes of KBS can be a fruitful way of easing the knowledge acquisition process which is generally accepted to be the bottleneck in the development of KBS.

The knowledge elicited from the expert is represented in the Expertise Model in GEMINI, which acts as a half-way house on the way to its incorporation in the KBS.

Dependence on experts

There are many factors which should be taken into account when choosing a suitable expert. In many cases the expertise which is required is not held by a single individual but must be acquired from several.

It is particularly important to use experts who have the ability to explain their problem-solving processes to people who are not specialists in their subject.

User interface requirements

KBS often require the user to provide information about the problem while using the system interactively. To do this effectively requires a greater emphasis on the user interface and the modes of use it supports than might be found in a conventional SSADM development.

Specialist tools

There are various high-level programming languages which are specifically suited to KBS development because they provide good support for symbolic as well as numeric manipulation. The most commonly used examples are LISP and Prolog. However, the use of these specialist languages has tended to decline and many KBS developments are now carried out using conventional languages. In addition to the programming languages, specialized tool kits and development environments are available and provide high productivity for suitable types of application.

5.2.2 The impact of KBS in an integrated system development

Assuming that the need for a KBS has been identified, it is important to assess those characteristics which will have an impact on the remainder of the development. Particular attention should be paid to this for the following reasons:

- KBS can place severe demands on processing and memory resources which may have an adverse effect on the performance of the non-KBS components if they are running on the same platform

- the mode of use of KBS is typically flexible and highly interactive.

The following should be considered:

- degree of user interaction with the KBS; this is addressed in the Modality Model in GEMINI

- size and associated performance demands likely to be imposed by the KBS

- criticality of the KBS:
  - how big a contribution does it make to the overall functionality of the system?
  - to what extent do the non-KBS components depend on the KBS to deliver their functionality?

5.2.3 Interfaces to KBS in an integrated system

In SSADM, the development of external interfaces is incremental, beginning with data flows to external entities, working through such products as Input/Output Structures, to complete dialogue design.

No such rigorous approach is offered by GEMINI but it is recommended in the *GEMINI Technical Reference*, section 7.6 that external interfaces should be defined prior to developing the Functional Design model.

# Chapter 5
## GEMINI and SSADM: working together

The knowledge-based parts of an integrated system can be treated in two ways:

- fully integrated as processes within the normal SSADM analysis and design

- moved outside the mainstream to an external position.

KBS as processes

As processes, the KBS are linked to the remainder of the system by data flows and may be associated with particular processes in data flow diagrams and functional definitions.

An example of such an application might be the creditworthiness KBS component within the banking cheque clearance system described in section 2.3. This is a component which applies expertise to assess the creditworthiness of customers whose accounts contain insufficient funds to cover a transaction. The component would be integrated within a conventional system which was transferring funds between cheque accounts and would exchange data flows with the other components of that system.

The integration of analysis and design products is managed in the same way as for non-KBS elements in SSADM. However, the KBS are developed separately using KBS techniques under GEMINI, since Enquiry and Update Process Models are unsuitable for describing the non-deterministic behaviour of KBS.

The Logical Data Model applies to both parts of the system if any of the data is to be used by the KBS. However, detailed problem-solving knowledge relevant only to the KBS will be entirely contained within the KBS processes. Where the KBS elements are large, their requirements may drive the data modelling activities.

During Technical System Options, careful consideration should be given to the processing needs of the KBS, since the inferencing processes of KBS may place high demands on both the CPU and memory. This will be an important consideration in Capacity Planning.

## GEMINI in an SSADM Environment – Developing KBS Components

**KBS as external entities**

As external entities, the KBS may be treated as 'users' of the system for integration purposes.

An example of such an application might be an advisory expert system which could be called from a holiday booking system to provide travel agency staff with on-line advice on the suitability of different holiday locations. It might access the same database of holiday details, but would otherwise take all its input from the user in response to questions about the customer.

In strict SSADM terms this means that the KBS is not part of the SSADM development. However, the decision to treat the KBS as an external entity may not be made until as late as Step 330 Function Definition, so its treatment is discussed here.

There are two ways of treating a KBS as an external entity:

- the KBS is treated as a separate entity, but with common user interface conventions. At the very least, it is likely that User Roles will be defined, with associated tasks

- the KBS is treated as another system. This means that its input/output requirements will be specified in I/O Descriptions and an External Entity Description will specify its function and the constraints on how it interfaces with the SSADM components.

For both cases, in order to consider integration as an external entity early in the development, Step 350 Develop Specification Prototypes can be modified to prototype the communications between the SSADM and KBS elements.

### 5.3 Where to identify KBS in the SSADM project lifecycle

It is important to consider the incorporation of KBS components as early as possible in the project. A successfully integrated project is likely to have considered KBS at the Feasibility Stage. If KBS are not identified until later in the project, it may be necessary to undertake an extra GEMINI feasibility study at that point. This will clearly have an impact on the timescales and dependencies of the overall project.

The following sections are structured around the SSADM Version 4 Stages and are intended to give pointers to where KBS should be considered and could possibly be identified.

## 5.3.1 Feasibility study

**020 Define the Problem**

During definition of the problem, an overview of the existing system is being produced, and an attempt should be made to identify business activities which require specialist skill or training for their performance.

Interviews carried out during this stage may identify the need to involve potential experts. An initial assessment of the applicability of KBS to the problems and requirements can be made.

Data Flow Diagram processes with complex Elementary Process Descriptions should be considered as candidates for KBS.

**030 Select Feasibility Options**

KBS can be identified as options for further investigation at this step. That investigation is likely to involve some initial knowledge acquisition activities.

The Feasibility Options produced should include different combinations of KBS elements. Rough cost estimates of the KBS can be made based on estimates of the amount and complexity of knowledge needed and these can contribute to the cost/benefit analysis.

## 5.3.2 Analysis

The analysis stages repeat much of the work done during the feasibility study in greater detail. As the conventional parts of the system are developed the interfaces to the KBS are refined.

**Stage 1: Investigation of Current Requirement**

Since this stage is comparable to Step 020 in the feasibility study, but more detailed, the same considerations apply. It may be that new problems or requirements are identified during this stage and the appropriateness of KBS to address them should be reconsidered.

# GEMINI in an SSADM Environment – Developing KBS Components

| | | |
|---|---|---|
| | Stage 2:<br>Business System Option | Since this stage is comparable to Step 030 of the feasibility study, but more detailed, the same considerations apply. |
| | Stage 3:<br>Definition of Requirements | The detailed analysis that takes place during this stage may bring to light areas suited to the application of a KBS approach. Much the same considerations as for Step 020 in the Feasibility Study apply. In addition, during Step 330 Define Systems Functions, more complex decision-making functions in particular should be considered as possible candidates for KBS. |
| | Stage 4:<br>Technical System Options | Since this stage is comparable to Step 030 of the feasibility study, but more detailed, the same considerations apply. |
| 5.3.3 | Logical and Physical Design (Stages 5 and 6) | If a KBS is not identified until the design stages in SSADM it is likely to have a serious impact on project costs and timescales unless it is exceptionally simple and well decoupled in a non-critical or optional part of the overall system. |
| 5.4 | **Interfaces in integrated projects** | The following general principles should be adopted in integrating GEMINI into an SSADM project: |

- The project is approached as an SSADM project and typically begins with an SSADM Feasibility Study. If, during the Feasibility Study, potential KBS are identified, these should be subjected to a further feasibility assessment along the lines recommended by GEMINI

- From this point on SSADM should be applied to all aspects of the project. However, it will be necessary to generate additional products specifically for the KBS components – see section 5.5.4

- Particular attention needs paying to the interfaces between the KBS and non-KBS components

- The analysis and design of the KBS and non-KBS components should be co-ordinated through the generation of the corresponding products (section 5.5.2). The activities which generate those products are defined in Stages and Steps in SSADM and are illustrated by an exemplar set of activities in GEMINI – see section 5.6.

## 5.5 Equating products from SSADM and GEMINI

The assumption in this section is that the SSADM development is acting as an umbrella for two branches of software development, KBS and non-KBS. In other words, SSADM is the overall method with GEMINI in support.

Many SSADM products may be useful in KBS elements of an SSADM project. Some GEMINI-specific Management Products and Technical Products may prove useful in the overall project. There are some GEMINI Technical Products which have no relevance to or equivalent in SSADM, but which are essential to the development of the KBS.

In addition, there are some products which cover aspects of analysis and design which are common to all system components. These are defined as **umbrella products** and are described in the section below.

### 5.5.1 Umbrella products

Some SSADM products will be usable on both KBS and non-KBS parts of the system. For instance it could be useful to have the User Catalogue as an umbrella product.

SSADM products which should be used as umbrella products, ie which will span the two branches of an integrated development are:

- Requirements Catalogue
- User Catalogue
- Data Catalogue
- Capacity Planning Input
- Application Style Guide
- Technical Environment Description.

The Current Services Description describes the business environment within which the proposed application(s) will be developed. This is encompassed by the Business Domain Model in GEMINI but for an integrated application the SSADM product may be sufficient.

To ease integration of development, including user testing, the Requirements Catalogue should cover the requirements for both parts of the development and all resolutions should be recorded in the Requirements Catalogue whether the resolution is in SSADM products or GEMINI ones.

The Data Catalogue provides definitions for all persistent data which is used by the SSADM components, whether for their sole use or for sharing information with the KBS. Entities which are required solely by the KBS need not be recorded in the Logical Data Model or in the SSADM Data Catalogue. Any attributes of shared entities which are only used by the KBS should be recorded.

Using the SSADM lifecycle as the basis for development activities, the Capacity Planning Input, Application Style Guide and Technical Environment Description are generated earlier than the equivalent products are developed under GEMINI. However, to ensure smooth integration of the SSADM and GEMINI components, it is recommended that, where practicable, the SSADM approach be used. This may necessitate extensive early prototyping of performance and user interface aspects of the KBS.

### 5.5.2 High-level product correspondences

There are several direct correspondences between the products recommended in the *GEMINI Technical Reference* and SSADM products. For instance, Activity Descriptions are used identically in each method. Figure 5.1 maps the analysis and design products of GEMINI on to the high-level products of SSADM. For each GEMINI product generated for a KBS component, it identifies the SSADM products which perform the same function for a non-KBS component. This enables the analysts to understand the use and purpose of the various GEMINI models. No temporal ordering is defined in GEMINI for the production of the models, as it is in SSADM.

| GEMINI products | SSADM Products |
|---|---|
| Feasibility Report | Feasibility Report |
| Business Domain Model | All Stage 1 products |
| Selected Application Model | Selected Business System Option |
| Application Requirements, and Logical Analysis Models | Requirements Specification |
| Expertise and Modality | No equivalent models |
| Technical Environment Description | Technical Environment Description |
| Functional Design Model | Logical Design |
| Physical Design Model | Physical Design |

Figure 5.1: Mapping the analysis and design products of GEMINI to the high-level products of SSADM

The mappings above are not meant to suggest that there are corresponding levels of workload involved in the production of the various products. The feasibility study for a KBS can be a much more protracted step than for conventional systems.

5.5.3 Low-level product correspondences

GEMINI suggests possible product compositions for all models, many of which utilize techniques specific to KBS development. Since no particular technique or product is prescribed at the level below the ten high-level products listed above, all SSADM low-level products (eg Logical Data Structures, Menu Structures, Data Flow Diagrams) are candidates for production of the KBS high-level products. More guidance on the choice of techniques for developing specific GEMINI products is given in Chapter 8 (particularly sections 8.5 and 8.6) of the *GEMINI Technical Reference*.

5.5.4 KBS-specific products

The Expertise Model, which contains a representation of the knowledge that the Expert feels is appropriate to the application, is specific to GEMINI but part of the model's composition might be SSADM products such as Data

# GEMINI in an SSADM Environment – Developing KBS Components

Flow Diagrams. Similarly the Modality model, which contains the user view of the knowledge-based application in terms of tasks to be performed, has no direct equivalent in SSADM, but products such as the User Catalogue and User Roles could be incorporated.

## 5.6 Relating SSADM and GEMINI activities

Activities in SSADM are defined explicitly and precisely, while allowing for tailoring. In GEMINI example activities are provided in broad outline only, requiring GEMINI practitioners to determine a set of activities which is suitable to their own development environment. The guidance in this section relates to the activity examples provided in *GEMINI Technical Reference*, Chapter 7. If any other route is taken through the GEMINI activities, then adaptation of this guidance will be required.

A simplified view of the mapping of SSADM modules to GEMINI activities is shown in Figure 5.2.

| GEMINI activities | SSADM Modules |
|---|---|
| Feasibility Study | Feasibility Study |
| Requirements Analysis System Modelling | Requirements Analysis |
| Logical Analysis | Requirements Specification |
| Logical Design, Technical Environment Definition | Logical System Specification |
| Physical Design | Physical Design |

Figure 5.2: The mapping of SSADM modules to GEMINI activities

Mapping from SSADM modules to GEMINI activities works only at a very high level. Closer inspection reveals that the production of the Expertise and Modality models, which correspond to no specific products in SSADM, have been included under the activity, Logical Analysis. This highlights the area where the mappings between the GEMINI and SSADM are weakest, ie the

# Chapter 5
## GEMINI and SSADM: working together

stages of development between analysis of the business domain and logical design.

It is advisable that the GEMINI activities focus only on the development of the KBS, ignoring mention in the GEMINI volumes of non-KBS considerations. For instance, in *GEMINI Technical Reference*, Chapter 7, Step SM.30 of the System Modelling activity is to identify the KBS and non-KBS elements of an integrated development, but if the overall project is being run under SSADM then this is done at the points stated in section 5.3.

Detail on GEMINI activities is given below to identify their likely impact on SSADM activities. Activities are included which, though entirely contained within GEMINI, will have significant impact on the non-KBS development.

### 5.6.1 GEMINI Feasibility

The GEMINI Feasibility Study in an integrated project should be concerned only with the feasibility of the possible KBS components. These may have been identified later than the initiation of the SSADM Feasibility Study. Using the example activities in *GEMINI Technical Reference*, section 7.2, the feasibility study should:

- in Step FS.30, provide a provisional schedule for the KBS development and assess this schedule in relation to the plan for the overall project

- in Step FS.46, assess the organizational feasibility of a KBS implementation. The use of KBS can have a significant impact on the way organizations use IT because of the high level of decision-making that the system undertakes. The costs and risks associated with a KBS development will be considered here. These will be evaluated against the potential benefits of cost reduction, and gain in service levels, competitive edge and improved performance. This may well impact on the SSADM development

- in Step FS.50, produce a feasibility report focused on the KBS bearing in mind integration with the non-KBS development.

### 5.6.2 GEMINI Requirements Analysis

As in the Feasibility Study, the focus is on the KBS elements of the integrated development. The business requirements are expected to be covered by SSADM, but if any additional business requirements are identified during GEMINI activities, they should be recorded in the SSADM Requirements Catalogue. Using the example activities in *GEMINI Technical Reference*, section 7.3, the Requirements Analysis stage should:

- in Step RA.20, identify any KBS user requirements in addition to those identified during SSADM requirements analysis. It is advisable to record all requirements in the SSADM Requirements Catalogue.

- in Step RA.30, expand the organizational requirements for the KBS, identified in the GEMINI feasibility study, in the context of the business requirements analysis for the overall project.

### 5.6.3 GEMINI System modelling

Using the example activities in *GEMINI Technical Reference*, section 7.4, Step SM.20 of System Modelling should identify and model all system-level data required by the KBS components.

Whether required solely for KBS purposes or not, any additional attributes of SSADM entities identified should be recorded in the SSADM Logical Data Model and Data Catalogue. These should be marked according to their use and may be subjected later to entity/event modelling to ensure they are adequately maintained.

### 5.6.4 GEMINI Logical Analysis

The Logical Analysis activity is specific to KBS within GEMINI so the steps to be completed are as given in *GEMINI Technical Reference*, section 7.5.

### 5.6.5 GEMINI Logical Design

Using the example activities in *GEMINI Technical Reference*, section 7.6, Step LD.30 of Logical Design should resolve the requirements for integration testing with the non-KBS components.

### 5.6.6 GEMINI Technical Environment Definition

Using the example activities in *GEMINI Technical Reference*, section 7.7, the Technical Environment Definition should select the technical environment for the implementation of the system. Any implications of this selection for the overall system, especially performance and capacity planning issues, should be available to the SSADM Technical System Options.

| 5.6.7 | GEMINI Physical Design | Using the example activities in *GEMINI Technical Reference*, section 7.8, the Physical Design should design the knowledge-based element of the integrated physical design. In particular, it should, in Step PD.20: |

- co-ordinate with the SSADM activities to detail system interfaces

- define the physical characteristics and form of the data to be input to and output from the KBS, co-ordinating with the SSADM physical data design where necessary.

| 5.7 | **Techniques on KBS projects** | KBS projects typically use a greater diversity of techniques than conventional system projects. GEMINI supports this diversity by providing a framework into which practitioners can fit the techniques they employ. Some of those techniques will be specialized KBS techniques, others will be derived from more generally applicable techniques, including some found in SSADM. |

| 5.8 | **Specialized KBS techniques** | The specialized KBS techniques are required to support the activities of knowledge acquisition knowledge representation and knowledge base validation. |

| 5.8.1 | Knowledge acquisition | *GEMINI Technical Reference*, section 8.2, describes a number of techniques which are specific to knowledge acquisition and which may be useful in the analysis and design of a KBS. However, it should be recognized that most of these are supplementary techniques used to support the basic technique of knowledge acquisition by dialogue with the Expert. For this, the primary skills required are those associated with communication and establishing a common basis of understanding. |

The basic process of knowledge acquisition can be characterized by the following idealized series of steps:

- in discussion with the Expert, the Knowledge Engineer obtains a degree of understanding of the subject area

- the Expert provides an initial description of the problem-solving process, from which they agree a form of intermediate representation which meets the following criteria:
    - it is understandable to both parties and can, therefore, act as a basis for communication
    - it can ultimately be transformed into an executable form

- the knowledge base is progressively built up in this representation

- the complete knowledge base is transformed into an executable form, retaining the intermediate form for the purposes of subsequent maintenance.

In practice this process involves many iterations and revisions, particularly in agreeing the most appropriate form of representation. However, it illustrates the type of informal and unstructured techniques and skills that are typically deployed.

If it proves useful, the process may be structured by employing more formal techniques. Some of those suggested and described in *GEMINI Technical Reference*, section 8.2, include:

- exploratory interviews

- structured interviews

- case analysis

- simulated work

- training

- questionnaires.

All of these may be useful under particular circumstances and can be used according to the personal preferences of the Knowledge Engineer.

Other knowledge acquisition aids

Other techniques are used either as acquisition aids or as the basis of agreeing a form of intermediate

# Chapter 5
## GEMINI and SSADM: working together

representation for the knowledge base with the Expert. They would typically be used either as preparation for interviews with the Expert, or if the Knowledge Engineer was experiencing difficulty in eliciting a particular aspect of the Expert's knowledge.

Techniques which the Knowledge Engineer might use to help establish and define the concepts used by experts include:

- repertory grids

- multidimensional scaling

- hierarchical clustering

- statistical- and machine-learning techniques such as rule induction, for deriving implicit knowledge from corporate data.

These are described in *GEMINI Technical Reference*, sections 8.2.1 and 8.2.3.

In preparation for knowledge acquisition sessions with the Expert, documentary sources may be a particularly cost-effective way of gaining access to expertise. *GEMINI Technical Reference*, section 8.2.2, suggests suitable sources and draws attention to possible pitfalls in its use.

Systems analysis in KBS

Systems analysis in KBS involves knowledge acquisition and representation to define certain aspects of the system to be produced, and as such overlaps heavily with conventional systems analysis. In practice KBS systems analysis should be seen as part of the overall systems analysis process, but addressing the mechanisms for achieving the required functionality in detail, where this is dependent on the direct emulation of human expertise.

In a KBS development, the rules by which a conclusion is reached are often complex and vary between different examples of the same problem. Systems analysis must therefore be extended beyond data and processes to analyse and formalize the problem-solving strategies and tactics used by the expert. This is the process of knowledge acquisition. It involves in-depth discussions with experts to elicit the knowledge that they use to tackle the problem and the representation of that knowledge in a form that is understandable to experts and capable of conversion into an executable program.

The relationship between systems analysis and knowledge acquisition may then be summarized thus:

- systems analysis is relevant to, and necessary for, all projects, whether KBS or otherwise

- knowledge acquisition should be viewed as an extension to conventional systems analysis which deals specifically with aspects of the functionality of the system which must be supplied by a domain expert

- knowledge acquisition involves the derivation of an appropriate form in which to represent the knowledge for subsequent incorporation in the system.

5.8.2 Knowledge representation

The purpose of knowledge acquisition is to analyse and document the expertise. The primary concern of any such documentation is that it should be immediately understandable by both the expert and the knowledge engineer. It cannot and should not be too restrictive or formalized. A standard notation would be useful to help with this process but is not currently available. In the meantime, *GEMINI Technical Reference*, section 8.3, describes the following techniques:

- production rules

- frames

- first order predicate logic

- representation of certainty

- contexts/worlds

- semantic nets and conceptual models

- qualitative models.

### 5.8.3 KBS validation

KBS present some particularly challenging validation problems, since it is necessary to validate the content of the knowledge base against the mental processes of the Expert or several experts.

This process cannot be left to system testing, but must be an ongoing activity throughout the development of the system. *GEMINI Technical Reference*, section 8.4, recommends appropriate techniques for verification and evaluation.

## 5.9 Generally applicable techniques

There are several generally applicable techniques which can be used on KBS development projects. They include general IT techniques such as prototyping, task analysis, and soft system methodology.

A number of SSADM techniques are also directly applicable and there are two aspects to the use of existing SSADM techniques and skills which need to be considered:

- SSADM techniques in GEMINI – how they can assist in the KBS part of the development

- GEMINI effects on SSADM techniques – the impact that the integration of the GEMINI KBS development will have on the use of SSADM techniques in the rest of the development.

### 5.9.1 SSADM techniques in GEMINI

Since KBS can incorporate conventional information modelling, it follows that many SSADM techniques are potentially useful in KBS development. It is, therefore, important to identify those likely to be useful in a high proportion of KBS developments and closely allied to specific KBS techniques.

Techniques such as logical data modelling and data flow modelling may be used frequently in KBS developments, whereas techniques such as enquiry process modelling are likely to be used only rarely.

### 5.9.2 GEMINI effects on SSADM techniques

Some SSADM techniques require modification in an integrated project. For example, an enriched data model may be necessary to reflect the more complex views of data required by KBS. Even if the Logical Data Model is

# GEMINI in an SSADM Environment – Developing KBS Components

used only for entities needed by the software being developed under SSADM, attributes belonging to such entities, required for KBS purposes only, could be recorded on the Entity Descriptions and highlighted as having non-SSADM use.

There may be a need to extend Entity Life Histories to show changes of attributes/state made by KBS components. To eliminate the inclusion of such effects in subsequent Effect Correspondence Diagrams and subsequent Update Process Models which as stated in section 5.2.3 are unsuitable for KBS, these effects must be differentiated from those resulting from 'normal' events. Depending on the extent of the effects of KBS processing on entities in the Logical Data Model, it may be necessary either to extend the concept of parallel lives to include a KBS life, or to introduce a symbol to identify KBS-related events.

Data flow modelling may need extension, when the KBS-as-process view is taken, in order to distinguish KBS processes from those processes to be developed using SSADM. Another approach could be to annotate the relevant Elementary Process Descriptions and Function Definitions.

Due to the highly interactive nature of decision-support in KBS, to maintain a common look and feel to both parts of the ultimate system, Application Style Guide, logical dialogue design and physical screen design must consider the requirements of the GEMINI development.

**5.10 Selection of techniques**

The KBS-specific techniques listed in *GEMINI Technical Reference*, sections 8.2–8.4, differ from SSADM techniques in that they are:

- less structured
- less closely related to products.

**5.10.1 Structure of KBS techniques**

SSADM techniques are well defined and highly structured. KBS techniques are far less structured.

These differences partly reflect a lack of maturity and standardization in KBS techniques, but are to a large extent due to the fundamental character of KBS.

KBS are concerned primarily with emulating human expertise in a software system. The form in which that knowledge is expressed by experts varies widely. The techniques used to elicit that knowledge must therefore remain unbounded until such time as it can be demonstrated that all human knowledge can be transformed into a finite set of representations. In the meantime, the Knowledge Engineer must be allowed flexibility to derive the most appropriate representation scheme, based on the nature of the expertise described by the domain expert.

5.10.2 Relationship to products

The close relationship between activities, techniques and products which exists in SSADM and which provides such valuable guidance to the practitioner is less prevalent in GEMINI.

*GEMINI Technical Reference*, section 8.6, provides an outline mapping of techniques on to the GEMINI models. However, the final selection of techniques must remain with the Project Manager, taking into account the nature of the requirements and any project-specific constraints such as the availability of specific skills and tool support.

In the absence of more definitive guidance it is important that the Project Manager should consider the widest range of techniques, make the basis of selection explicit and critically review the basis on which the decisions were made.

# 6 Skills requirements

## 6.1 Introduction

This chapter provides guidance on the skills needed on an integrated KBS development that is carried out under SSADM and GEMINI. Most of the skills required are those associated with any software development project. However, there are requirements for specialized skills in three areas:

- the Project Controller role
- project management
- knowledge engineering.

## 6.2 Project Controller

The Project Controller has a wide range of responsibilities and tasks requiring a combination of management skills and awareness of the technical issues likely to affect KBS developments.

Individuals who undertake this role require training and experience in:

- resource management
- quality concepts
- project management
- KBS technology
- human factors management.

They also need to obtain a deep understanding of the significance of the proposed development within the organization, for example:

- the user issues, including the way in which the system will be used and the user functions likely to be affected
- the utilization and control of specialized knowledge within the business
- the business implications of the new system.

# GEMINI in an SSADM Environment – Developing KBS Components

- the constraints imposed by the IS strategy

The Project Controller ideally has previous experience of deploying GEMINI.

## 6.3 Project management

There are three main areas in which the presence of a KBS component being developed according to GEMINI affects the project management of a conventional system development. These are:

- risk assessment
- control of iterative development
- management of the expert.

### Risk assessment

Since KBS developments still represent the application of relatively new technology, there tends to be greater uncertainty and risk associated with them than with conventional information systems development. The GEMINI approach recognizes this and encourages a more explicit consideration of risk at each stage. Experience of the management of risk is needed within the project management organization, preferably of using GEMINI to develop KBS.

### Control of iterative development

The activities of analysis, design and implementation tend to overlap in KBS development to a degree not normally expected in conventional systems development. Models are developed in parallel using an iterative approach. Control of this iterative development requires experience in using the GEMINI project management process model or a similar type of spiral lifecycle model.

### Management of the Expert.

Since a KBS project is likely to depend on the use of experts as the source of the knowledge to be incorporated into the KBS, skills in this area tend to be critical to a successful KBS development. The Knowledge Engineer may carry out day to day interaction with the Expert but the Project Controller controls the Expert and the rest of the Domain Team and the Project Manager must ensure that best use is made of the time it spends contributing to the development. The Expert is very often the critical resource in the project and every possible step must be taken to maximize their

# Chapter 6
# Skills requirements

commitment and ensure that sufficient of their time is made available to service the demands of the KBS development.

**6.4 Knowledge engineering**

The prime requirements for the role of Knowledge Engineer are excellence in both information gathering through interviews, and analysis of the findings. The Knowledge Engineer is concerned not only with eliciting facts and procedures but also the reasoning processes which experts apply to such facts and procedures. This requires good listening skills as well as the ability to make explicit the thought processes which experts use intuitively.

**6.4.1 Transfer of SSADM skills**

Since KBS can incorporate conventional information modelling, many of the SSADM techniques are potentially useful in KBS development. The level of usefulness of SSADM products will vary from project to project. In many projects logical data modelling will be useful with some extension for the specialist nature of expert knowledge, while any SSADM product which takes a highly structured view of processing will be less useful, eg Logical Update Process Models.

**6.4.2 Special KBS skills**

While some SSADM techniques will be relevant to the tasks of the Knowledge Engineer, other techniques are specific to KBS developments and special training is required before experience can be gained on a KBS development team. While there may be scope for such experience to be gained within an integrated project, the use of KBS techniques must be under the control of a KBS practitioner.

The acquisition and representation of knowledge from the expert is the activity that most distinguishes KBS development from other system development. To transfer from SSADM analysis to knowledge engineering, the principal skills required are those involved in:

- information gathering through interviews, for the purposes of knowledge acquisition

- the interpretation of the findings, for the purposes of knowledge representation.

The Knowledge Engineer is concerned not only with eliciting facts and procedures but also with the reasoning processes which the expert applies to such facts and procedures. This requires good listening skills as well as the ability to make explicit the thought processes which experts use intuitively.

Some of the techniques which are available to assist in the knowledge acquisition activity are listed in Chapter 8 of the volume *GEMINI Technical Reference*. Experience in the use of a range of these techniques is required by Knowledge Engineers.

Knowledge Engineers need an understanding of the constraints imposed by the various representation schemes available to encode the knowledge they acquire. They also need experience of selecting and applying these representation schemes.

### 6.4.3 Training for Knowledge Engineers

The key qualities to look for when deciding who is suitable for training in GEMINI/KBS techniques are the abilities to listen and then to model the underlying structure of the information given. These are general skills required by good systems analysts. However, they are of particular importance to Knowledge Engineers.

Above all the Knowledge Engineer must be a pragmatist. KBS often involve incremental development with no clear cut off point; a pragmatic approach prevents the process from iterating in pursuit of an unnecessarily high degree of perfection. Important qualities are the ability to decide which part of the expert knowledge will contribute most to the problem being addressed and the ability not to be side-tracked by interesting but irrelevant detail.

Given the required personal qualities, there are two specific topics in which training is required:

- knowledge representation

- knowledge acquisition.

The training should be provided in that order. General training in knowledge acquisition will be difficult without a few basic techniques for representing the results of acquisition. The training in knowledge representation should provide guidelines on when and how to use specific techniques. This must be mastered before the concepts and application of acquisition techniques are provided. A knowledge engineer should have both skills.

In addition to general KBS training, some training will be required in the GEMINI approach to KBS development, in particular the various models.

Ideally only experienced knowledge engineers are used in an integrated development, especially if the KBS development team is small. Newly trained knowledge engineers may be used if they are given sufficient support from experienced staff and timescales are flexible enough.

Any training should ideally take place before the start of the project, preferably before KBS development work starts, since the feasibility study phase of the GEMINI part requires the greater part of the KBS effort (see section 3.2.2). If training is delayed the SSADM part of the development may suffer severe delays.

6.4.4 Sources of knowledge engineering training

There are several sources of knowledge engineering training:

- universities

- institutes affiliated to universities

- software suppliers who provide training in subjects related to their products and services

- commercial training establishments

- consultancies.

University-led courses provide a good theoretical grounding, while other training establishments often take a more pragmatic approach. No training is likely to equip staff to undertake KBS tasks without a significant amount of supervision from an experienced knowledge engineer.

In addition to detailed training in knowledge acquisition and representation techniques, management overviews are provided by the classes of training supplier given in the previous paragraph and give a basic understanding of the issues involved in the application of KBS technology.

# Annex

# A  Object-orientation and KBS

**A.1  Introduction**

Despite the many features which distinguish KBS from other types of system, recent developments in software engineering have created overlaps.

Software systems increasingly address significant applications which are inevitably complex, since the application domains which they model are themselves complex, eg manufacturing production scheduling, satellite tracking systems etc. At the same time, they must be reliable, maintainable and extendable.

Because of the need to be able to model the complexity which is inherent in many application domains, there are trends in general software development towards approaches which provide different types of model for applications. The most prevalent and influential of these in relation to potential KBS applications is object-orientation.

**A.2  Object-orientation**

The object-oriented paradigm is an approach to modelling which builds on ideas of abstract (real world) objects, encapsulation and class inheritance.

- An **object** contains both data, represented by attributes, and processing, represented by methods. The 'object' behaves (performs a task) in response to receiving a message that it understands

- A **method** is an internally coded procedure which implements (part of) the functionality of an object. It is actioned when the object receives a specific message

- Encapsulation, also known as **information hiding**, ensures that the internal structure of an object is invisible to all other objects. Encapsulation isolates the object data and methods from the outside world. All communication between objects is in the form of messages

- A **message** is the mechanism by which one object communicates with another to force the execution of a method

- **A class** is used to define common attributes and methods for a group of objects. The 'class object' can be considered as a parent of the (child) objects it relates to. A child may have more than one parent

- **Inheritance** is the hierarchic mechanism by which 'child' objects exhibit behaviour and properties defined by their forebears.

Most software design methods approach complexity by decomposing the problem into manageable units. Object-orientation differs from other approaches in the way that it performs decomposition. In object-orientation, the world is modelled as a collection of objects, which have relationships to each other and which interact to carry out tasks. This model is proving to be a powerful way of handling complexity. Moreover, it seems to provide a model which is intuitively closer to a user's view of the world.

## A.3 Object-orientation and GEMINI

Both object-orientation and declarative knowledge representation in KBS model the domain of the application and it is not surprising that there are many similarities. The concept of an 'object' corresponds closely with that of a 'frame' in KBS and concepts such as inheritance and encapsulation are common to both approaches. Rich modelling techniques in KBS were adopted because of the need to model the concepts and processes involved in human reasoning and problem solving.

KBS and object-orientation diverge when it comes to modelling the problem-solving processes in the system. Object-orientation makes no assumptions about the nature of those processes, but in most cases they are based on algorithms generated by the software designers themselves. In KBS, the problem-solving processes use expertise in the application domain and are typically (but not exclusively) represented as rules. Dependence on experts for the problem-solving knowledge in a system is a criterion for using GEMINI.

Distinguishing features of GEMINI are:

- management of risk

- use of specialized techniques for acquiring and representing expert knowledge

- an iterative lifecycle model.

Object-orientation may help to reduce risk in a GEMINI sub-project because it is a well-defined technique which encourages the management of decomposition in a way that enables the behaviour of discrete *chunks* of an application to be dealt with independently. This eases maintenance, which is a particular problem in KBS because of their dynamic nature.

GEMINI may be useful for the derivation of an object model which requires extensive interaction with an expert.

An iterative type of project management process model is frequently appropriate for object oriented developments.

Section 3.7 of this publication gives some guidance on ways of applying various GEMINI concepts.

The object-oriented approach must be adopted as a conscious decision on the part of the design team. It may be particularly useful where a component of an SSADM project, which has been identified as being on the borderlines of KBS, displays characteristics which make it tractable to object-oriented techniques. In such a case SSADM needs tailoring in a way which is outside the scope of this publication; some guidance can be found in the publications; *Customizing SSADM* and *Managing Reuse*.

# Bibliography

**Information Systems Engineering Library**

The Information Systems Engineering Library provides guidance on managing and carrying out Information Systems Engineering activities. Relevant publications:

- Customizing SSADM
  ISBN: 0 11 330664 4

- Managing Reuse
  ISBN: 0 11 330616 4

- Prototyping in an SSADM Environment
  ISBN: 0 11 330582 6

**GEMINI**

The foundation volumes of the GEMINI guidance consisting of three volumes:

- GEMINI: Controlling KBS Development Projects – Guidance for business-side project controllers
  ISBN: 0 11 330591 5

- GEMINI: Managing KBS Development Projects – Guidance for IS-provider project managers
  ISBN: 0 11 330592 3

- GEMINI Technical Reference – Guidance for KBS development project teams
  ISBN: 0 11 330593 1

# Glossary

Where terms are specific to either SSADM or GEMINI, this is indicated in italics.

activity
: The process of creation, or further development, of a product. Each time a product is to be created or enhanced, an activity is defined to effect the transformation.

Activity Network *(SSADM)*
: Places all of the activities into logical sequence, thus enabling timescales to be estimated and work to be scheduled.

Analysis of Requirement *(SSADM)*
: This forms the Module Product from the Requirements Analysis Module. It consists of the Current Services Description, Requirements Catalogue, User Catalogue and the Selected Business System Option.

Application Requirements Model *(GEMINI)*
: The product that holds a specification of the required external behaviour of the system, together with the organizational, operational, technical and resource constraints which affect the way that the system is to be designed and implemented.

attribute *(SSADM)*
: A characteristic property of an entity type, that is, any detail that serves to describe, qualify, identify, classify, quantify or express the state of an entity. If possible the logical attributes for an entity will be translated directly into data items within the physical representation. An attribute may be optional for an entity, meaning that it does not apply to all occurrences of the entity.

Business Domain Model *(GEMINI)*
: The product that provides an understanding of the organizational structure and business functions. This understanding allows the scope of possible applications to be identified. The impact of a possible system on the organization can be clarified and defined. For potential applications the Business Domain Model covers both current and proposed systems and requirements.

Business System Options *(SSADM)*
: Stage 2 in SSADM. The aim is to take the Requirements Catalogue, Current Services Description and User Catalogue and use this information as the basis on which

## Using GEMINI in an SSADM Environment – Developing KBS Components

|  |  |
|---|---|
| | to decide the most appropriate way for development to meet the business needs. This Stage has Two Steps:<br><br>210 – Define Business System Options<br>220 – Select Business System Option. |
| capacity planning | Used to predict the (hardware/software) configuration required to satisfy the constraints and requirements of the proposed system. It is also used to assist in the development of service level agreements (outside SSADM). |
| Data Catalogue *(SSADM)* | The central repository for all the descriptive information about items of data. This includes physical details which may be found during data flow modelling activities as well as physical design activities. Logical data modelling will provide information about attributes (the logical equivalent to data items). |
| Data Flow Diagram *(SSADM)* | Shows how services are organized and processing is undertaken. It should be a simple diagram that is readily understood, so that it can act as an effective means of communication between analysts and users. |
| Data Flow Model *(SSADM)* | A set of Data Flow Diagrams and their associated documentation. The diagrams form a hierarchy with the Data Flow Diagram Level 1 showing the scope of the system and the lower-level diagrams expanding the detail as appropriate. Additional documentation provides a description of the processes, input/output data flows and external entities. |
| data flow modelling *(SSADM)* | Is used to help define the scope of the system and ensure that the analysts have a clear understanding of the user's problems and requirements. The technique is used to build a model of the information flows and not to define the detail of the processing performed by the system. |
| deliverables | Products which must be developed by the supply side and formally accepted by the demand side. These products must be defined in terms of content, structure and format. |

# Glossary

| | |
|---|---|
| Development Team | The team responsible for developing the products of specific development activities within a project. |
| dialogue design *(SSADM)* | A technique used to define the on-line activity of the system. Dialogues are identified as part of the Requirements Specification and then logically designed explicitly as part of the Logical Design. Physical dialogue design activities are undertaken during the physical design activities to complete the design prior to system implementation. |
| Domain Team *(GEMINI)* | The team responsible for providing information for use in analysis and design activities. The team is made up of the User and Expert roles. |
| Effect Correspondence Diagram *(SSADM)* | Shows all the affects an event has on data within the system and how those effects impact upon each other. Effect Correspondence Diagrams provide the access path details for update functions which is used in logical design activities. |
| entity *(SSADM)* | Is something, whether concrete or abstract, which is of importance to the area of business being investigated. Logical data modelling identifies types of entity, not individual occurrences: ie **Tenant** and **Applicant** not **John Smith**. |
| Entity Life History *(SSADM)* | Charts all of the events that may cause a particular entity to be changed in any way. It shows the valid structure of events (initially identified through use of data flow modelling and function definition techniques) affecting an entity on the Logical Data Structure. |
| Exception Plan | The product which documents the details of an exception situation which has arisen, or is likely to arise, including extremes that have been examined or considered and proposes corrective action. |
| expert | A person who has detailed understanding in the domain of knowledge for which the KBS is to be designed. The role, **Expert**, is undertaken by a group of experts, or their representative, who provide information, during analysis and design, by interviews or by documentary evidence such as manuals or case studies. |

| | |
|---|---|
| Expertise Model *(GEMINI)* | The product which holds a structured description of the knowledge (expertise) to be encoded into the implemented KBS. |
| external entity *(SSADM)* | Is a source or recipient (or both) of data which exists outside the boundary of the defined system but which communicates with the system. An external entity may be another system, an organization, an individual or a group of people. These are documented within the Data Flow Model. |
| Feasibility *(SSADM)* | Stage 0 in SSADM. The objective is to investigate the requirements laid down within the Project Initiation Document and suggest the way ahead. This Stage has four Steps:<br><br>010 – Prepare for the Feasibility Study<br>020 – Define the problem<br>030 – Select Feasibility Options<br>040 – Assemble Feasibility Report. |
| Feasibility Study (FS) *(GEMINI)* | This activity generates an initial assessment of the feasibility of building a system in the area of business which has been identified by a strategy study or project review activities. |
| Feasibility Study Module *(SSADM)* | The Module whose objective is to produce the Feasibility Report which will suggest the way ahead for the project. The activities form a short assessment of a proposed information system to determine whether the system would be feasible and appropriate to the business needs of the organization. Feasibility is assessed in terms of the managerial, business, financial, technological and cultural needs of the organization. This Module has one Stage:<br><br>Stage 0 – Feasibility. |
| Function Definition *(SSADM)* | Is the description of the function and provides a cross-reference to other associated SSADM products. |
| Functional Design Model *(GEMINI)* | The product which reflects design decisions concerning how individual components of the system will be implemented. It is a revision of the Logical Analysis Model. |

# Glossary

| | |
|---|---|
| knowledge acquisition | A term commonly applied to the process by which KBS project teams gain an understanding of the knowledge in the business area of concern. |
| knowledge based systems (KBS) | Computer systems which are characterized by their ability to hold and make available knowledge in a specific domain. |
| Knowledge Engineer *(GEMINI)* | The role of development personnel in a KBS project. They carry out the analysis, design and programming activities for a KBS development. |
| knowledge representation | The formalisms that are adopted to record expertise in a structured form. |
| Logical Analysis (LA) *(GEMINI)* | This activity specifies precisely what is needed to meet the requirements without being constrained by how the requirements are to be met. |
| Logical Analysis Model *(GEMINI)* | The pivotal product in a GEMINI-based project. It brings together the Expertise Model and the Modality Model into a single validated whole. |
| Logical Data Model *(SSADM)* | Provides an accurate model of the information requirements of all or part of an organization. Serves as a basis for file and database design, but is independent of any specific implementation technique or product. The Logical Data Model consists of a Logical Data Structure, Entity Descriptions and Relationship Descriptions. Associated descriptions or attribute/data items and grouped domains are maintained in the Data Catalogue. |
| Logical Design (LD) *(SSADM/GEMINI)* | The term Logical Design is used in both SSADM and GEMINI. In both cases, the activity completes and checks all aspects of the design before implementation issues are considered in Physical Design. |

Logical Design is Stage 5 in SSADM. The aim is to take the Requirements Specification and further develop the processing requirements in such a way as to be implementation independent prior to physical design activities. This Stage has four Steps:

510 – Define User Dialogues
520 – Define Update Processes

93

530 – Define Enquiry Processes
540 – Assemble Logical Design

Modality Model *(GEMINI)* — Defines interactions in the proposed system. **Agents** are persons or processes that interact with or are components of the proposed system. The Modality Model identifies the agents, defines which tasks each performs and how they can exchange information. The pattern of interaction between agents is termed **modality**.

object orientation — The object-oriented paradigm is an approach to modelling which builds on ideas of abstract (real world) objects, encapsulation and class inheritance.

- An **object** contains both data, represented by attributes, and processing, represented by methods. The 'object' behaves (performs a task) in response to receiving a message that it understands

- A **method** is an internally coded procedure which implements (part of) the functionality of an object. It is actioned when the object receives a specific message

- **Encapsulation**, also known as 'information hiding', ensures that the internal structure of an object is invisible to all other objects. Encapsulation isolates the object data and methods from the outside world. All communication between objects is in the form of messages

- A **message** is the mechanism by which one object communicates with another to force the execution of a method

- A **class** is used to define common attributes and methods for a group of objects. The 'class object' can be considered as a parent of the (child) objects it relates to. A child may have more than one parent

- **Inheritance** is the hierarchic mechanism by which 'child' objects exhibit behaviour and properties defined by their forebears.

See Booch (1991), Meyer (1988) and Rumbaugh (1991).

# Glossary

| | |
|---|---|
| Physical Design (PD) *(SSADM / GEMINI)* | The term Physical Design is used in both SSADM and GEMINI. In both cases, this activity generates the Physical Design Model in sufficient detail to enable development of the operational system.

Physical design is Stage 6 in SSADM. The objective is to specify the physical data and physical processes using the language and features of the chosen implementation environment and incorporating installation standards. This Stage has seven Steps:

    610 – Prepare for Physical Design
    620 – Create Physical Data Design
    630 – Create Function Component Implementation Map
    640 – Optimize Physical Data Design
    650 – Complete Function Specification
    660 – Consolidate Process Data Interface
    670 – Assemble Physical Design |
| Physical Design Model *(GEMINI)* | The product which represents all the components and functions of the system to be implemented. It is implementation dependent, the design details being dependent on the technical environment chosen for implementation. |
| plan | The product that documents the results of the planning process. It shows targets in terms of products, resources required, timescales and quality. It shows how the resources identified have been scheduled to meet these targets. |
| planning | The process of estimating, collating, sequencing and scheduling the project's resources to deliver the required products. |
| PRINCE | A government developed method for project management with particular application to the management of Information Systems projects. It is a development of the PROMPT method which has been in use in government departments since 1983. |
| product | Any output from a project. The output may be an item of software, hardware or documentation and may itself consist of a number of detailed products. In GEMINI, |

|  |  |
|---|---|
|  | products are described within three main categories: *Management Products* (which are produced during the management of a project), *Technical Products* (which are those products that make up the system) and *Quality Products* (which are produced for, or by, the quality process). |
| product description | The product which describes the purpose, form and components of a product, and lists the quality criteria which apply to it. |
| Product Flow Diagram (PFD) | The product which is used to describe the technical strategy of a project in terms of a diagram showing the products of the project and how they are derived from each other. It is essentially a working document produced by planners for their own benefit. |
| Project Board | A group of senior managers within the demand side organization who have an interest in, and overall control of, the KBS project. The Project Board must provide overall guidance and direction to the project. The Project Board comprises:<br><br>• Executive<br><br>• Senior User<br><br>• Senior Technical. |
| Project Controller *(GEMINI)* | The demand side project manager responsible for the success of the project in terms of the quality of the delivered system, budget and timescale. The Project Controller acts on behalf of the Project Board, has close links with the board members and attends board meetings. |
| project management process model *(GEMINI)* | An iterative approach to project management for KBS development projects. This model incorporates four sectors concerning the activities of risk assessment, planning, development and review. |
| Project Manager *(GEMINI)* | A role with day-to-day responsibility for ensuring that the supply side produces the required products, to the required standard of quality, within specified constraints of time and cost. |

# Glossary

| | |
|---|---|
| project organization | The composition of a project team in terms of the skills and experience required to undertake all of the necessary functions of control, management and development within a project. |
| QA | See quality assurance. |
| quality | Quality is defined in ISO 8402 as: |

*the totality of features and characteristics of a product or service that bear on its ability to satisfy stated or implied needs.*

| | |
|---|---|
| quality assurance (QA) | The scope of quality assurance is described in ISO 8402–1986. It covers: |

*all those planned and systematic actions that provide adequate confidence that a product or service will satisfy given requirements for quality.*

| | |
|---|---|
| quality criteria | The identifiable characteristics of a product that are to be examined to determine whether the product meets stated requirements and can be considered fit for its purpose. These characteristics are documented in a product description for each product. |
| Requirements Analysis (RA) (SSADM/GEMINI) | The term Requirements Analysis is used in both SSADM and GEMINI. In both cases, this activity specifies requirements early in the project to establish a sound basis for design and acceptance. |
| Requirements Analysis Module (SSADM) | The objective is to produce the Analysis of Requirements. Within this the Selected Business System Option will define the scope of further investigation. This Module has two Stages:<br><br>Stage 1 – Investigation of Current Environment<br>Stage 2 – Business System Options. |
| Requirements Catalogue (SSADM) | Is the central repository for information covering all identified requirements, both functional and non-functional. Each entry is textual and describes a required facility or feature of the proposed system. |

| | |
|---|---|
| Requirements Specification Module *(SSADM)* | The objective is to produce the Requirements Specification. This Module has one Stage:<br><br>    Stage 3 – Definition of Requirements. |
| Risk *(GEMINI)* | In a GEMINI project, **risk** is the likelihood, and impact, of a project **failing** to:<br><br>• meet a business need and provide expected business benefits<br><br>• prove technically feasible<br><br>• prove organizationally feasible<br><br>• complete on time and within budget<br><br>• develop products which meet requirements. |
| risk assessment | The process of identifying risks, evaluating their impact and identifying countermeasures. |
| role | One of the discrete project functions required to manage and carry out a project. Roles are assigned to individuals according to the needs of the project and the mix of skills available. |
| Selected Application Model *(GEMINI)* | The product which provides a representation of the tasks and data flows in an application. This representation provides a more precise definition of the functionality of the proposed application than the Business Domain Model. |
| spiral model | see project management process model. |
| Stage *(SSADM)* | The SSADM framework requires a subject to be subdivided into a number of Modules each of which consists of one or more Stages. A Stage is a unit of activity with a single goal and rationale. Each Stage of one or more Steps has a defined set of products and activities. |
| System Modelling (SM) *(GEMINI)* | This activity defines the business environment around the proposed application in detail so that the application impact on the business can be established accurately. |

# Glossary

| | |
|---|---|
| Team Leader *(GEMINI)* | Responsible for managing a Development Team and specific resources during the development of particular products. |
| Technical Environment Definition (TE) *(GEMINI)* | This activity generates a detailed assessment of the technical environment for implementation of the application. |
| Technical Environment Description (TED) *(SSADM/GEMINI)* | This product contains a definition of the requirements of the environment in which the application is to be developed and will run. |
| Technical System Options *(SSADM)* | SSADM Stage 4, aims is to take the Requirement Specification and decide on the most appropriate way for development to meet the technical needs. This Stage has two Steps:<br><br>410 – Define Technical System Options<br>420 – Select Technical System Options. |
| Update Process Model (UPM) *(SSADM)* | Is a structure diagram for the update (event) processing and the associated operations list. This is based on the Entity Life Histories, which provide a data-oriented view of the system, and the associated Effect Correspondence Diagrams, which provide an event-oriented or process-oriented view of the system. |
| user *(GEMINI)* | Any person who uses a system for business purposes. The role, **User**, is undertaken by a group of users, or their representative, who provides information, during analysis and design, on user requirements and may be involved in testing. |

# Index

activity (ies)  9, 25, 31, 33-36, 38, 39, 42-51, 53, 54, 64-67, 73, 89-93, 95, 97-99
agent (s)  32, 94
Application Products  31, 32
Application Requirements Model  32, 33, 63, 89
Application Style Guide  61, 62, 72
Artificial Intelligence  11
Business Domain Model  32, 33, 62, 63, 64, 89, 98
Business System Options  60, 89, 90, 97
capacity planning  8, 57, 61, 62, 67, 90
Capacity Planning Input  61, 62
case analysis  68
cognitive psychology  54
conceptual models  70
configuration management  37, 51
contexts  70
control points  29-31, 30, 42, 43, 45, 47, 48, 50
cost estimates  59
Current Services Description  61, 89
Data Catalogue  61, 62, 66, 90, 93
Data Flow Diagram  17, 59, 88
Data Flow Model  90, 92
data flow modelling  71, 72, 90, 91
data processing  19, 54
declarative knowledge  13, 84
Definition of Requirements  60, 96
deliverables  29, 30, 32, 50, 90
demand side  25, 27, 28, 41, 90, 96
Development Team  20, 28, 41, 77, 79, 91, 99
dialogue Design  56, 72, 91
Domain Team  27, 28, 76, 91
Effect Correspondence Diagram  91
Elementary Process Descriptions  17, 59, 72
entity (ies)  56, 58, 62, 66, 72, 89, 90, 91-93, 99
Entity Life History (ies)  72, 91, 99
estimating  91, 95
Exception Plan  42, 91
Exception Report  50
expert system  11, 58
expertise  11, 12, 14, 17-20, 32, 33, 54, 55, 57, 63, 64, 69, 70, 73
Expertise Model  32, 33, 55, 63, 92, 93
exploratory interviews  68

external entity  58, 92
external interfaces  56
Feasibility Options  59, 92
Feasibility Report  33, 63, 65, 98
Feasibility Stage  48, 58
Feasibility Study  17, 25, 33, 35, 38, 43, 46, 48, 50, 59, 60, 63, 64, 65, 66, 79, 92
Feasibility Study Module  92
first order predicate logic  70
frames  70
Function Definition  58, 92
Functional Design  33, 56, 63, 92
GEMINI
    example activities  64-67
    product  31-33, 39, 47, 50, 51, 61-63, 89, 91-99
hierarchical clustering  69
Human-Computer Interaction  93
I/O Descriptions  58
identification of a KBS  50
inference engine  14, 20, 23
Input/Output Structures  56
interfaces  53, 54, 56, 58, 59, 60, 67
intermediate representation  68
Investigation of Current Requirement  59
Iterative development  35, 37, 76
Knowledge acquisition  12, 18, 21-23, 34, 38, 39, 46, 48, 54, 55, 59, 67, 68, 69, 70, 77-80, 93
Knowledge base  14, 18, 20, 21, 52, 67, 68, 69, 71
KBS as an external entity  58
KBS as processes  57
KBS validation  14, 34, 67, 71
Knowledge Engineer  28, 40, 41, 67, 68, 69, 70, 73, 76-80, 93
knowledge engineering  75, 77, 79
knowledge representation  12, 14, 18, 34, 37, 67, 70, 77-79, 82, 93
LISP  55
Logical Analysis  32, 33, 43, 64, 66, 92, 93
Logical Analysis Model  32, 33, 63, 92, 93
Logical Data Model  57, 62, 66, 71, 72, 93
Logical Data Structure  91, 93
Logical Design  33, 43, 63-66, 91, 93, 94
management controls  37, 50
management products  31, 51, 61, 96
memory resources  56

modality  32, 33, 56, 63, 64, 93, 94
Modality Model  32, 33, 56, 64, 93, 94
multidimensional scaling  69
object-orientation  23, 81-83, 94
organizational requirements  66
partial products  51
Physical Data Design  67, 95
Physical Design  33, 43, 60, 63, 64, 67, 90, 91, 93, 95
Physical Design Model  33, 63, 95
plan  29, 42-45, 47, 48, 65, 91, 95
planning  8, 29, 31, 36, 37, 38, 42-46, 48, 50, 57, 61, 62, 67, 90, 95, 96
PRINCE  7, 9, 27, 28, 30, 31, 33, 35, 36, 37, 39, 42-46, 50, 51, 95
problem-solving knowledge  11, 13, 57, 84
process models  37, 57, 72, 77
product controls  50
product description  50, 96, 97
Product Flow Diagram  39, 96
production rules  70
Project Board  27, 28, 41, 50, 96
project control  25, 31, 37, 38, 50
Project Controller  27, 28, 31, 27, 40, 41, 75, 76, 96
project management  7, 25, 29, 30, 37, 39, 41, 42, 44, 75, 76, 85, 95, 96, 98
project management process model  25, 29, 42, 44, 76, 83, 96, 98
Project Manager  9, 27, 28, 41, 42, 73, 76, 96
project organization  25, 26, 97
project plan (s)  29, 42, 48
project planning  37, 42, 46, 46
project products  43, 51
Prolog  55
prototyping  41, 51, 52, 55, 62, 71
QA  97
qualitative models  70
quality  27, 30, 31, 37, 41-43, 50, 51, 75, 95-97
quality control  50, 97
quality criteria  50, 51, 96, 97
quality management  97
questionnaires  68
re-planning  29, 37, 38, 46, 48
repertory grids  69
representation of certainty  70
Requirements Analysis  33, 43, 64, 66, 89, 97

Requirements Analysis Module 89, 97
Requirements Catalogue 47, 61, 62, 66, 89, 97
Requirements Specification Module 98
Resource Plan 42
Review 29, 31, 36, 44, 50, 73, 92, 96
Risk Analysis 38, 45, 48
risk assessment 29, 31, 36, 37, 44, 50, 76, 96, 98
risk management 51, 98
roles 26-28, 36, 37, 40, 45, 58, 64, 91, 98
rule induction 69
scheduling 46, 81, 95
Selected Application Model 32, 33, 63, 98
semantic nets 70
simulated work 68
Spiral lifecycle model 38, 76
spiral model 44, 98
SSADM products 36, 45, 46, 48, 50, 51, 61, 62, 63, 77, 92
Stage (s) 8, 9, 30, 31, 36, 42, 46, 48, 58-60, 63, 89, 90, 92, 93, 95, 97-99
Step (s) 34, 45, 51, 58-60, 65, 66, 67, 90, 92, 93, 95, 98, 99
structured interviews 68
supply side 25, 27, 28, 90, 96
System Modelling 33, 43, 64, 65, 66, 98
Systems analysis 54, 69, 70
Team Leader 28, 42, 95
Technical Environment 33, 43, 61, 62, 63, 64, 66, 95, 99
Technical Environment Definition 33, 64, 66, 99
Technical Environment Description 43, 61, 62, 63, 99
technical plan 42, 43
technical products 31, 51, 61, 96
Technical System Options 48, 57, 60, 67, 99
techniques 8, 9, 12, 14, 21-23, 25, 34-36, 37-40, 53, 54, 57, 63, 67-73, 77-80, 84, 85, 90
telephone link test 19
tool kits 56
tools 34, 54, 55
training 8, 9, 59, 68, 75, 77-80
Umbrella products 61
Update Process Model 99
User Catalogue 61, 64, 89
user interface 52, 54, 55, 58, 62
user requirements 66, 95
validation 14, 34, 67, 71
where to identify KBS 53, 58
worlds 70

Printed in the United Kingdom for HMSO
Dd299887 2/95 C6 G3397 10170